TECHNOLOGY AND SOCIETY

TECHNOLOGY AND SOCIETY

Advisory Editor
DANIEL J. BOORSTIN, author of
The Americans and Director of
The National Museum of History
and Technology, Smithsonian Institution

MEMOIR

OF

ELI WHITNEY, ESQ.

BY

DENISON OLMSTED

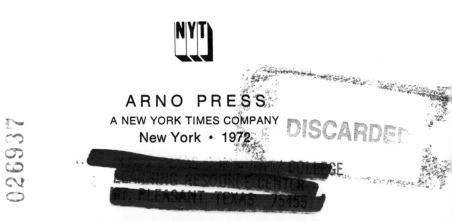

ARNO PRESS
A NEW YORK TIMES COMPANY
New York • 1972

Reprint Edition 1972 by Arno Press Inc.

Reprinted from a copy in The Pennsylvania
State Library

Technology and Society
ISBN for complete set: 0-405-04680-4
See last pages of this volume for titles.

Manufactured in the United States of America

―――――――――

Library of Congress Cataloging in Publication Data

Olmsted, Denison, 1791-1859.
  Memoir of Eli Whitney, Esq.

  (Technology and society)
  Reprint of the 1846 ed.
  1. Whitney, Eli, 1765-1825. I. Series.
TS1570.W404 1972   681'.7631'0924 [B]   72-5065
ISBN 0-405-04716-9

MEMOIR

OF

ELI WHITNEY, ESQ.

BY

DENISON OLMSTED,

PROFESSOR OF NATURAL PHILOSOPHY AND ASTRONOMY, YALE COLLEGE.

First published in the American Journal of Science, for 1832.

NEW HAVEN:

DURRIE & PECK.

PECK & STAFFORD, PRINTERS.

1846.

CONTENTS.

MEMOIR.

THE memory of the late Mr. Whitney is so fondly cherished by his fellow citizens, out of respect to his distinguished talents, his private virtues, and his public spirit, and his name holds so honorable a place among the benefactors of our country, that the wish has often been intimated to us of seeing a more extended biography of him, than has hitherto been given to the public.

We now enter with pleasure upon such a task ; and to enable us to do the better justice to the subject, we have been favored with access to his extensive correspondence, and to all his other writings, and have conferred freely with various persons, who were long and intimately acquainted with him.

ELI WHITNEY was born at Westborough, Worcester County, Massachusetts, December 8, 1765. His parents belonged to the middle class in society, who, by the labors of husbandry, managed, by uniform industry and strict frugality, to provide well for a rising family. From the same class have arisen most of those who, in New England, have attained to high eminence and usefulness ; nor is any other situation in society so favorable to the early formation of those habits of economy, both of time and money, which, when carried forward into the study of the scholar, or the field of active enterprise, afford the surest pledge of success.

The paternal ancestors of Mr. Whitney emigrated from England among the early settlers of Massachusetts, and their descendants were among the most respectable farmers of Worcester County. His maternal ancestors, of the name of FAY, were also English emigrants, and ranked among the substantial yeomanry of Massachusetts. A family tradition respecting the occasion of their coming to this country, may serve to illustrate the history of the times. The story is, that,

1

about two hundred years ago, the father of the family, who resided in England, a man of large property and great respectability, called together his five sons and addressed them thus : " America is to be a great country ; I am too old to emigrate to it myself; but if any one of you will go, I will give him a double share of my property." The youngest son instantly declared his willingness to go, and his brothers gave their consent. He soon set off for the New World, and landed at Boston, in the neighborhood of which place he purchased a large tract of land, where he enjoyed the satisfaction of receiving two visits from his venerable father. His son, *John Fay*, from whom the subject of this memoir is immediately descended, removed from Boston to Westborough, where he became the proprietor of a large tract of land, since known by the name of the *Fay-Farm.*

From Mrs. B., the sister of Mr. Whitney, we have derived some particulars respecting his childhood and youth, and we shall present the anecdotes to our readers in the artless style in which they are related by our correspondent, believing that they would be more acceptable in this simple dress, than if, according to the modest suggestion of the writer, they should be invested with a more labored diction. The following incident, though trivial in itself, will serve to show at how early a period certain qualities of strong feeling, tempered by prudence, for which Mr. Whitney afterwards became distinguished, began to display themselves. When he was six or seven years old, he had overheard the kitchen-maid, in a fit of passion, calling his mother, who was in a delicate state of health, hard names, at which he expressed great displeasure to his sister. " She thought (said he) that I was not big enough to know any thing ; but I can tell her, I am too big to hear her talk so about by mother. I think she ought to have a flogging, and if I knew how to bring it about, she should have one." His sister advised him to tell their father. " No, (he replied,) that will not do ; it will hurt his feelings and mother's too : and besides, it is likely the girl will say she never said so, and that would make a quarrel. It is best to say nothing about it."

Indications of his mechanical genius were likewise developed at a very early age. Of his early passion for such employments, his sister gives the following account. "Our father had a workshop, and sometimes made wheels, of different kinds, and chairs. He had a variety of tools, and a lathe for turning chair-posts. This gave my brother an opportunity of learning the use of tools when very young. He lost no time ; but as soon as he could handle tools he was always making something in the shop, and seemed not to like working on the farm. On a time, after the death of our mother, when our father had been absent from home two or three days, on his return, he inquired of the housekeeper, what the boys had been doing? She told him what B. and J. had been about. But what has Eli been doing? said he. She replied, he has been making a fiddle. 'Ah! (added he despondingly,) I fear Eli will have to take his portion in fiddles.' He was at this time about twelve years old. His sister adds, that this fiddle was finished throughout, like a common violin, and made tolerably good music. It was examined by many persons, and all pronounced it to be a remarkable piece of work for such a boy to perform. From this time he was employed to repair violins, and had many nice jobs, which were always executed to the entire satisfaction, and often to the astonishment, of his customers. His father's watch being the greatest piece of mechanism that had yet presented itself to his observation, he was extremely desirous of examining its interior construction, but was not permitted to do so. One Sunday morning, observing that his father was going to meeting, and would leave at home the wonderful little machine, he immediately feigned illness as an apology for not going to church. As soon as the family were out of sight, he flew to the room where the watch hung, and taking it down, he was so delighted with its motions, that he took it all in pieces before he thought of the consequences of his rash deed ; for his father was a stern parent, and punishment would have been the reward of his idle curiosity, had the mischief been detected. He, however, put the work all so neatly together, that his father never discovered his audacity until he himself told him, many years afterwards."

Whitney lost his mother at an early age, and when he was thirteen years old, his father married a second time. His step-mother, among her articles of furniture, had a handsome set of table knives, she valued very highly, which our young mechanic observing, said to her, 'I could make as good ones, if I had tools, and I could make the necessary tools, if I had a few common tools to make them with.' His step-mother thought he was deriding her, and was much displeased ; but it so happened not long afterwards, that one of the knives got broken, and he made one exactly like it in every respect, except the stamp on the blade. This he would likewise have executed, had not the tools required been too expensive for his slender resources.

When Whitney was fifteen or sixteen years of age, he suggested to his father an enterprise, which was an earnest of the similar undertakings in which he engaged on a far greater scale in later life. This being the time of the Revolutionary war, nails were in great demand, and bore a high price. At that period, nails were made chiefly by hand, with little aid from machinery. Young Whitney proposed to his father to procure him a few tools, and to permit him to set up the manufacture. His father consented, and he went steadily to work, and suffered nothing to divert him from his task, until his day's work was completed. By extraordinary diligence, he gained time to make tools for his own use, and to put in knife blades, and to perform many other curious little jobs, which exceeded the skill of the country artisans. At this laborious occupation, the enterprising boy wrought alone, with great success, and with much profit to his father, for two winters, pursuing the ordinary labors of the farm during the summers. At this time he devised a plan for enlarging his business and increasing his profits. He whispered his scheme to his sister, with strong injunctions of secrecy : and requesting leave of his father to go to a neighboring town, without specifying his object, he set out on horseback in quest of a fellow laborer. Not finding one so easily as he had anticipated, he proceeded from town to town, with a perseverance which was always a strong trait of his character, until at the distance of forty miles from home, he found such a workman às he desired. He also made his journey subservient to his improvement in mechanical skill, for he called at every workshop on his way, and gleaned all the information he could respecting the mechanic arts.

At the close of the war, the business of making nails was no longer profitable ; but a fashion prevailing among the ladies of fastening on their bonnets with long pins, he contrived to make those with such skill and dexterity, that he nearly monopolized the business, although he devoted to it only such seasons of leisure as he could redeem from the occupations of the farm, to which he now principally betook himself. He added to this article, the manufacture of walking canes, which he made with peculiar neatness.

In respect to his proficiency in learning, while young, we are informed that he early manifested a fondness for figures, and an uncommon aptitude for arithmetical calculations, though in the other rudiments of education, he was not particularly distinguished. Yet, at the age of fourteen, he had acquired so much general information, as to be regarded, on this account, as well as on account of his mechanical skill, a very remarkable boy.

From the age of nineteen, young Whitney conceived the idea of obtaining a liberal education ; but being warmly opposed by his step-mother, he was unable to procure the decided consent of his father, until he had reached the age of twenty three years. But, partly by the avails of his manual labor, and partly by teaching a village school, he had been so far able to surmount the obstacles thrown in his way, that he had prepared himself for the Freshman class in Yale College, which he entered in May, 1789. An intelligent friend and neighbor of the family helped to dissuade his father from sending him to college, observing, that "it was a pity such a fine mechanical genius as his should be wasted ;" but he was unable to comprehend how a liberal education, by enlarging his intellectual powers and expanding his genius, would so much exalt those powers and perfect that genius, as to place their possessor among the Arkwrights of the age, while without such means of cultivation, he might have been only an ingenious millwright or blacksmith. While a schoolmaster, the mechanic would often usurp the place of the teacher ; and the mind, too aspiring for such a sphere, was wandering off in pursuit of perpetual motion. While at home in the month of July, 1788, making arrangements to go to New Haven, for the purpose of entering college, he was seized with a violent fever attended by a severe cough, which threatened to terminate his life. At length the disease centered in one of his limbs. A painful swelling, extending to the bone, ensued, which was finally relieved by surgical operation. After his recovery, he went to Durham, in Connecticut, and finished his preparation for college, under the care of that eminent scholar, Rev. Dr. Goodrich. As we are soon to accompany Mr. Whitney beyond the sphere of his domestic relations, we may mention here, that he finished his collegiate education with little expense to his father. His last college bills were indeed paid by him, but the money was considered as a loan, and for it the son gave his note, which he afterwards duly canceled. After the decease of his father, he took an active part in the settlement of the estate, but generously relinquished all his patrimony for the benefit of the other members of the family.

We have already mentioned that Mr. Whitney entered Yale College at the mature age of twenty three years. He had enjoyed but little intercourse with men of learning, and the state of elementary education, in the part of the country where he passed his minority, was unfavorable to his acquiring a knowledge of polite literature ; and while a member of college, he seems to have devoted more attention to the mathematics, and especially to mechanics, theoretical as well as practical, than to the ancient classics. Among his files are found most or all of the compositions and disputations which he wrote during this period, commencing with 1789. The compositions are frequently characterized by great vividness of imagination, and the disputations by sound and correct reasoning. At this time of life, indeed, Mr. Whitney exhibited an imagination somewhat poetical ; his prose compositions had something of this vein, and he occasionally wrote verses. The written disputations found among his papers, are more than twenty in number. Some of them were read before the President, (the late Dr. Stiles,) and others were exhibited in the literary society to which he belonged. Their titles indicate the topics that were agitated by the students of that day. The subjects discussed were oftener political than literary. The writers partook largely of the enthusiasm which pervaded all ranks of our countrymen. They exulted in their release from a foreign yoke, and boasted of the victory they had achieved over British arms. They extolled the matchless wisdom of the new government, and contrasted its free spirit with the tyranny of most of the governments of the old world, and its youthful vigor with those mouldering fabrics. With a spirit somewhat prophetical, they anticipated the decline and overthrow of all arbitrary governments, and the substitution in their place, of a purely representative system, like our own, and thus maintained, (what is now even more probable than it was then,) that this government was set up to be a model to all the nations of the earth.

The propensity of Mr. Whitney to mechanical inventions and occupations, was frequently apparent during his residence at college. On a particular occasion, one of the tutors happening to mention some interesting philosophical experiment, regretted that he could not exhibit it to his pupils, because the apparatus was out of order, and must be sent abroad to be repaired. Mr. Whitney proposed to undertake this task, and performed it greatly to the satisfaction of the Faculty of the college.

A carpenter being at work upon one of the buildings of the gentleman with whom Mr. Whitney boarded, the latter begged permission to use his tools during the intervals of study; but the mechanic being a man of careful habits, was unwilling to trust them with a student, and it was only after the gentleman of the house had become responsible for all damages, that he would grant the permission. But Mr. Whitney had no sooner commenced his operations, than the carpenter was surprised at his dexterity, and exclaimed, " there was one good mechanic spoiled when you went to college."

Soon after Mr. Whitney took his degree, in the autumn of 1792, he entered into an engagement with a Mr. B., of Georgia, to reside in his family as a private teacher. On his way thither, he was so fortunate as to have the company of Mrs. Greene, the widow of General Greene, who, with her family, was returning to Savannah, after spending the summer at the north. At that time it was deemed unsafe to travel through our country without having had the small-pox, and accordingly Mr. W. prepared himself for the excursion, by procuring inoculation while in New York. As soon as he was sufficiently recovered, the party set sail for Savannah. As his health was not fully re-established, Mrs. Greene kindly invited him to go with the family to her residence at Mulberry Grove, near Savannah, and remain until he was recruited. The invitation was accepted; but lest he should not yet have lost all power of communicating that dreadful disease, Mrs. Greene had white flags (the meaning of which was well understood) hoisted at the landing, and at all the avenues leading to the house. As a requital for her hospitality, her guest procured the virus and inoculated all the servants of the household, more than fifty in number, and carried them safely through the disorder.

Mr. Whitney had scarcely set his foot in Georgia, before he was met by a disappointment which was an earnest of that long series of adverse events which, with scarcely an exception, attended all his future negotiations in the same State.* On his arrival, he was informed that Mr. B. had employed another teacher, leaving Whitney entirely without resources or friends, except those whom he had made in the family of Gen. Greene. In these benevolent people, however, his case excited much interest, and Mrs. Greene kindly said to him, my young friend, you propose studying the law; make my house your home, your room your castle, and there pursue what studies you please. He accordingly commenced the study of law under that hospitable roof.

Mrs. Greene was engaged in a piece of embroidery in which

---

* In a letter to his friend, Josiah Stebbins, Esq., (the late Judge Stebbins of Maine,) dated Geo., April 11, 1793, Mr. Whitney says, " Fortune has stood with her back towards me ever since I have been here."—It does not appear that so far as related to Georgia, he ever found her position reversed.

she employed a peculiar kind of frame called a *tambour*. She complained that it was badly constructed, and that it tore the delicate threads of her work. Mr. Whitney, eager for an opportunity to oblige his hostess, set himself at work and speedily produced a tambour frame made on a plan entirely new, which he presented to her. Mrs. Greene and her family were greatly delighted with it, and thought it a wonderful proof of ingenuity.*

Not long afterwards, a large party of gentlemen came from Augusta and the Upper country, to visit the family of Gen. Greene, consisting principally of officers who had served under the General in the Revolutionary army. Among the number were Major Bremen, Major Forsyth, and Major Pendleton. They fell into conversation upon the state of agriculture among them, and expressed great regret that there was no means of cleaning the green seed cotton, or separating it from its seed, since all the lands which were unsuitable for the cultivation of rice, would yield large crops of cotton. But until ingenuity could devise some machine which would greatly facilitate the process of cleaning, it was in vain to think of raising cotton for market. Separating one pound of the clean staple from the seed was a day's work for a woman; but the time usually devoted to picking cotton was the evening, after the labor of the field was over. Then the slaves, men, women and children, were collected in circles with one whose duty it was to rouse the dozing and quicken the indolent. While the company were engaged in this conversation, " gentlemen (said Mrs. Greene,) apply to my young friend, Mr. Whitney— he can make any thing." Upon which she conducted them into a neighboring room, and showed them her tambour frame, and a number of toys which Mr. W. had made, or repaired for the children. She then introduced the gentlemen to Whitney himself, extolling his genius and commending him to their

---

* Several years afterwards, his partner, Mr. Miller, writes to Mr. Whitney, " I presume your skill in mechanics is likely to give you employment enough with the ladies; for your name is often coupled with work-frames, needles, &c. &c. ; so that I apprehend you will ultimately be compelled to become ignorant and unskilful in these things, in your own defence."

notice and friendship. He modestly disclaimed all pretensions to mechanical genius ; and when they named their object, he replied that he had never seen either cotton or cotton seed in his life. Mrs. G. said to one of the gentlemen, " I have accomplished my aim. Mr. Whitney is a very deserving young man, and to bring him into notice was my object. The interest which our friends now feel for him, will, I hope, lead to his getting some employment to enable him to prosecute the study of the law."

But a new turn that no one of the company dreamed of, had been given to Mr. Whitney's views. It being out of season for cotton in the seed, he went to Savannah and searched among the warehouses and boats, until he found a small parcel of it. This he carried home, and communicated his intentions to Mr. Miller, who warmly encouraged him, and assigned him a room in the basement of the house, where he set himself at work with such rude materials and instruments as a Georgia plantation afforded. With these resources, however, he made tools better suited to his purpose, and drew his own wire, (of which the teeth of the earliest gins were made,) an article which was not at that time to be found in the market of Savannah. Mrs. Greene and Mr. Miller were the only persons ever admitted to his workshop, and the only persons who knew in what way he was employing himself. The many hours he spent in his mysterious pursuits, afforded matter of great curiosity and often of raillery to the younger members of the family. Near the close of the winter, the machine was so nearly completed as to leave no doubt of its success.

Mrs. Greene was eager to communicate to her numerous friends the knowledge of this important invention, peculiarly important at that time, because then the market was glutted with all those articles which were suited to the climate and soil of Georgia, and nothing could be found to give occupation to the negroes, and support to the white inhabitants. This opened suddenly to the planters boundless resources of wealth, and rendered the occupations of the slaves less unhealthy and laborious than they had been before.

Mrs. Greene, therefore, invited to her house gentlemen from different parts of the State, and on the first day after they had assembled, she conducted them to a temporary building, which had been erected for the machine, and they saw with astonishment and delight, that more cotton could be separated from the seed in one day, by the labor of a single hand, than could be done in the usual manner in the space of many months.

Mr. Whitney might now have indulged in bright reveries of fortune and of fame; but we shall have various opportunities of seeing, that he tempered his inventive genius with an unusual share of the calm, considerate qualities of the financier. Although urged by his friends to secure a patent, and devote himself to the manufacture and introduction of his machines, he coolly replied, that on account of the great expense and trouble which always attend the introduction of a new invention, and the difficulty of enforcing a law in favor of patentees, in opposition to the individual interests of so large a number of persons as would be concerned in the culture of this article, it was with great reluctance that he should consent to relinquish the hopes of a lucrative profession, for which he had been destined, with an expectation of indemnity either from the justice or the gratitude of his countrymen, even should the invention answer the most sanguine anticipations of his friends.

The individual who contributed most to incite him to persevere in the undertaking, was *Phineas Miller*, Esq. Mr. Miller was a native of Connecticut, and a graduate of Yale College. Like Mr. Whitney, soon after he had completed his education at college, he came to Georgia as a private teacher, in the family of Gen. Greene, and after the decease of the General, he became the husband of Mrs. Greene. He had qualified himself for the profession of law, and was a gentleman of cultivated mind and superior talents; but he was of an ardent temperament, and therefore well fitted to enter with zeal into the views which the genius of his friend had laid open to him. He had also considerable funds at command, and proposed to Mr. Whitney to become his joint adventurer, and to be at the whole expense of maturing the invention until it should be patented. If the machine should succeed in its intended operation, the parties agreed, under legal formalities, " that the profits and advantages arising therefrom, as well as all privileges and emoluments to be derived from patenting, making, vending, and working the same, should be mutually and equally shared between them." This instrument bears date May 27, 1793, and immediately afterwards they commenced business, under the firm of *Miller & Whitney.*

An invention so important to the agricultural interest, (and, as has proved, to every department of human industry,) could not long remain a secret. The knowledge of it soon spread through the State, and so great was the excitement on the subject, that multitudes of persons came from all quarters of the State to see the machine ; but it was not deemed safe to gratify their curiosity until the patent-right had been secured. But so determined were some of the populace to possess this treasure, that neither law nor justice could restrain them—they broke open the building by night and carried off the machine. In this way the public became possessed of the invention ; and before Mr. Whitney could complete his model and secure his patent, a number of machines were in successful operation, constructed with some slight deviation from the original, with the hope of evading the penalty for violating the patent-right.

As soon as the copartnership of Miller & Whitney was formed, Mr. Whitney repaired to Connecticut, where, as far as possible, he was to perfect the machine, obtain a patent, and manufacture and ship for Georgia such a number of machines as would supply the demand.

Within three days after the conclusion of the copartnership, Mr. Whitney having set out for the north, Mr. Miller commenced his long correspondence relative to the Cotton Gin.* The first letter announces that encroachments upon their rights had already commenced. " It will be necessary (says Mr. Miller) to have a considerable number of gins made, to be in readiness to send out as soon as the patent is obtained, in order to satisfy the absolute demand, and make people's heads

---

* This name was not applied by the inventor, but became such by popular use.

easy on the subject ; *for I am informed of two other claimants for the honor of the invention of cotton gins, in addition to those we knew before."*

On the 20th of June, 1793, Mr. Whitney presented his petition for a patent to Mr. Jefferson, then Secretary of State ; but the prevalence of the yellow fever in Philadelphia, (which was then the seat of government,) prevented his concluding the business relative to the patent, until several months afterwards. To prevent being anticipated, he took however the precaution to make oath to the invention before the Notary Public of the city of New Haven, which he did on the 28th of October, of the same year.

Mr. Jefferson, who had much curiosity in regard to mechanical inventions, took a peculiar interest in this machine, and addressed to the inventor an obliging letter, desiring farther particulars respecting it, and expressing a wish to procure one for his own use. Mr. Whitney accordingly sketched the history of the invention, and of the construction and performances of the machine. " It is about a year (says he) since* I first turned my attention to constructing this machine, at which time I was in the State of Georgia. Within about ten days after my first conception of the plan, I made a small, though imperfect model. Experiments with this encouraged me to make one on a larger scale ; but the extreme difficulty of procuring workmen and proper materials in Georgia, prevented my completing the larger one until some time in April last. This, though much larger than my first attempt, is not above one third as large as the machines may be made with convenience. The cylinder is only two feet two inches in length, and six inches diameter. It is turned *by hand,* and requires the strength of one man to keep it in constant motion. It is the stated task of one negro to clean fifty weight, (I mean fifty pounds after it is separated from the seed,) of the green seed cotton per day."—In the same letter Mr. Jefferson assured Mr. Whitney, that a patent would be granted as soon as the model was lodged in the Patent Office. In mentioning the favorable

---

* This letter is dated Nov. 24, 1793.

notice of **Mr.** Jefferson to his friend Stebbins, he adds, with characteristic moderation, *I hope, by perseverance, I shall make something of it yet.*

At the close of this year, (1793,) Mr. Whitney was to return to Georgia with his cotton gins, and Mr. Miller had made arrangements for commencing business immediately after his arrival. The plan was to erect machines in every part of the cotton district, and engross the entire business themselves. This was evidently an unfortunate scheme. It rendered the business very extensive and complicated, and as it did not at once supply the demands of the cotton growers, it multiplied the inducements to make the machines in violation of the patent. Had the proprietors confined their views to the manufacture of the machines, and to the sale of patent rights, it is probable they would have avoided some of the difficulties with which they afterwards had to contend. The prospect of making suddenly an immense fortune by the business of ginning, where every third pound of cotton (worth at that time from twenty five to thirty three cents) was their own, presented great and peculiar attractions. Mr. Whitney's return to Georgia was delayed until the following April. The importunity of **Mr.** Miller's letters, written during the preceding period, urging him to come on, evinces how eager the Georgia planters were to enter the new field of enterprise, which the genius of Whitney had laid open to them. Nor did they, at first, *in general*, contemplate availing themselves of the invention unlawfully. But the minds of the more honorable class of planters were afterwards deluded by various artifices, set on foot by designing men, with the view of robbing Mr. Whitney of his just right. To these we shall advert more particularly hereafter.

One of the greatest difficulties experienced by men of enterprise, at the period under review, was the extreme scarcity of money. In order to carry on the manufacture of cotton gins, and to make advances in the purchase of cotton, and establishments for ginning, to an extent in any degree proportioned to their wishes, Miller & Whitney required a much greater capital than they could command; and the sanguine temperament of Mr. Miller was constantly prompting him to advance in hazards, much farther than the more cautious spirit of Mr. Whitney would follow. But even the latter found it necessary sometimes to borrow money at an enormous interest. The first loan (for two thousand dollars) was made on terms which were deemed at that time peculiarly favorable; yet the company were to pay five per cent. premium in addition to the lawful interest. This was in 1794. In consequence of the numerous speculations in new lands into which so many of our countrymen were deluded, and the want of confidence created by the very application for a loan, the pressure for money was continually increasing. In 1796, Mr. Whitney applied to a friend in Boston to raise money for him on a loan, and received the following reply: " I applied to one of those vultures called brokers, who are preying on the purse-strings of the industrious, and was informed that he can procure the sum you wish at a premium of twenty per cent. on the following conditions, viz: You must make over and deposit with him public securities, such as funded stock, bank stock, or any kind of State notes, or Connecticut reservation land certificates, sufficient, at the going prices, fully to secure the debt and premium." In a more embarrassed state of Mr. Miller's private affairs, several years afterwards, he paid the enormous interest of five, six, and even seven per cent. *per month.*

We have said that the loan contracted by Mr. Whitney, in 1794, at a premium of five per cent. in addition to the lawful interest, was regarded as peculiarly favorable ; this is evident from the fact that, during the same year, Mr. Miller urges him to contract a new loan, if possible, for three thousand dollars, at twelve or fourteen per cent. provided it could be extended over a year.

In July, 1794, Mr. Whitney was confined by a severe illness, from which he recovered slowly ; but his business received a still farther interruption from a very fatal sickness, (the scarlet fever,) which prevailed in New Haven during this year, and which attacked a number of his workmen.

Under all these discouragements, Mr. Miller was constantly writing the most urgent letters from Georgia, to press forward the manufacture of machines. "Do not let a deficiency of money, do not let any thing (says Mr. Miller) hinder the speedy construction of the gins. The people of the country are almost running mad for them, and much can be said to justify their importunity. When the present crop is harvested, there will be a real property of at least fifty thousand, yes, of a hundred thousand dollars, lying useless, unless we can enable the holders to bring it to market. Pray remember that we must have from fifty to one hundred gins between this and another fall,* if there are any workmen in New England, or in the Middle States, to make them. In two years we will begin to take long steps up hill, in the business of patent ginning, fortune favoring."

The general resort of the planters to the cultivation of cotton, and its consequent production in vast quantities, the value of which depended entirely upon the chance of getting it cleaned by the gin, created great uneasiness, which first displayed itself in this pressure upon Miller & Whitney, and afterwards afforded great encouragement to the marauders upon the patent-right, who were now becoming numerous and audacious.

The *roller gin* was at first the most formidable competitor with Whitney's Machine. It extricated the seeds by means of rollers, crushing them between revolving cylinders, instead of disengaging them by means of teeth. The fragments of seeds which remained in the cotton, rendered its execution much inferior in this respect to Whitney's gin, and it was also much slower in its operation. Great efforts were made, however, to create an impression in favor of its superiority in other respects, to which we shall advert by and by.

But a still more formidable rival appeared early in the year 1795, under the name of the *Saw Gin*. It was Whitney's gin, except that the teeth were cut in circular rims of iron, instead of being made of wires, as was the case in the earlier forms of the patent gin. The idea of such teeth had early occurred to Mr. Whitney, as he afterwards established by legal proof. But they would have been of no use except in connection with the other parts of his machine; and, therefore, this was a pal-

---

* This letter is dated Oct. 26, 1794.

pable attempt to evade the patent-right, and it was principally in reference to this, that the lawsuits were afterwards held.

In March, 1795, in the midst of these perplexities and discouragements, Mr. Whitney went to New York, on business, and was detained there three weeks, by an attack of fever and ague, the seeds of which had been sown the previous season in Georgia. As soon as he was able to leave the house, he embarked on board a packet for New Haven. On his arrival at this place, he was suffering under one of those chills which precede the fever. As was usual, on the arrival of the packet, people came on board to welcome their friends, and to exchange salutations, when Mr. Whitney was informed that on the preceding day *his shop, with all his machines and papers, had been consumed by fire !* Thus, suddenly, was he reduced to absolute bankruptcy, having debts to the amount of four thousand dollars, without any means of making payment. Mr. Whitney, however, had not a spirit to despond under difficulties and disappointments, but was aroused by them to still more vigorous efforts.

Mr. Miller, also, on hearing of this catastrophe, manifested a kindred spirit. The letters written by Mr. Whitney on the occasion, we have not been able to obtain ; but the reply of Mr. Miller indicates what were the feelings of both parties. It may be of service to enterprising young men, who meet with misfortunes, to read an extract or two.

" I think with you, (says Mr. M.,) that we ought to meet such events with equanimity. We have been pursuing a valuable object by honorable means ; and I trust that all our measures have been such as reason and virtue must justify. It has pleased Providence to postpone the attainment of this object. In the midst of the reflections which your story has suggested, and with feelings keenly awake to the heavy, the extensive injury we have sustained, I feel a secret joy and satisfaction, that you possess a mind in this respect similar to my own— that you are not disheartened—that you do not relinquish the pursuit—and that you will persevere, and endeavor at all events to attain the main object. This is exactly consonant to my own determinations. I will devote all my time, all my thoughts, all my exertions, and all the money I can earn or borrow, to encompass and complete the business we have undertaken ; and if fortune should, by any future disaster, deny us the boon we ask, we will at least deserve it. It shall never be said that we have lost an object which a little perseverance could have attained. I think, indeed, it will be very extraordinary, if two young men, in the prime of life, with some share of ingenuity, with a little knowledge of the world, a great deal of industry, and a considerable command of property, should not be able to sustain such a stroke of misfortune as this, heavy as it is."

After this disaster the company began to feel much straightened for want of funds. Mr. Miller expresses a confidence that they should be able to raise money *in some way or other*, though he knows not how. He recommends to Mr. Whitney to proceed forthwith to erect a new shop, and to recommence his business ; and requests him to tell the people of New Haven, who might be disposed to render them any service, that they required nothing but a little time to get their machinery in motion, before they could make payment, and that the loan of money at *twelve per cent.* per annum would be as great a favor as they could ask. But, he adds, " in doing this, use great care to avoid giving an idea that we are in a *desperate situation*, to induce us to borrow money. To people who are deficient in understanding, this precaution will be extremely necessary ; men of sense can easily distinguish between the prospect of large gains and the approaches to bankruptcy. Such is the disposition of man, (he observes on another occasion,) that while we keep afloat, there will not be wanting those who will appear willing to assist us ; but let us once be given over, and they will immediately desert us."

While struggling with these multiplied misfortunes, intelligence was received from England, which threatened to give a final blow to all their hopes. It was, that the English manufacturers condemned the cotton cleaned by their machines, on the ground that *the staple was greatly injured*. On the receipt of this intelligence, Mr. Miller writes as follows : " This stroke of misfortune is much heavier than that of the fire, unless the impression is immediately removed. For, with that which now governs the public mind on this subject, our patent would be worth extremely little. Every one is afraid of the cotton. Not a purchaser in Savannah will pay full price for it. Even the merchants with whom I have made a contract for purchasing, begin to part with their money reluctantly. The trespassers on our right only laugh at our suits, and several of the most active men are now putting up the roller gins ; and, what is to the last degree vexing, many prefer their cotton to ours."

At this time, (1796,) Miller & Whitney had thirty gins, at eight different places in the State of Georgia, some of which were carried by horses or oxen, and some by water. A number of these were standing still for want of the means of supplying them. The company had also invested about $10,000 in real estate, which was suited only to the purposes of ginning cotton. All things now conspired to threaten them with deep insolvency. Under date of April 27th, Mr. Miller writes thus : " A few moments only are allowed me to tell you, that the industry of our opponents is daily increasing, and that prejudices appear to be rapidly extending themselves in London against our cotton. Hasten to London, if you return immediately—our fortune, our fate depends on it. The process of patent ginning is now quite at a stand. I hear nothing of it, except the condolence of a few real friends, who express their regret that so promising an invention has entirely failed."

Through nearly the whole of the year 1796, Mr. Whitney was on the eve of departing for England, whither he was going with the view of learning the certainty of the prejudices, which were so currently reported to be entertained by the English manufacturers against the cotton cleaned by the patent gin, and the fame of which was so industriously circulated throughout the southern papers ; and should he find these prejudices to exist, firmly believing, as the event has shown, that they were utterly unfounded, he hoped to be able to remove them by challenging the most rigorous trials. He had several times fixed on the day of his departure, and on one occasion had actually engaged his passage and taken leave of some of his friends. But he was in each case thwarted by an unexpected disappointment in regard to the funds necessary to defray the expenses of the journey.

Mr. Whitney had counted on obtaining one thousand dollars for this purpose, through the aid of Mr. John C. Nightingale, who, having married a daughter of Mrs. Miller, had become interested in their concerns. Mr. Nightingale had inherited a considerable fortune, but had become greatly embarrassed by speculations in the Yazoo lands. He had, however, some credit left, while neither Miller nor Whitney, nor both together, had credit enough to borrow a thousand dollars. The plan was, therefore, for Nightingale to borrow the money and lend it to them ; and Miller urges this, even at the rate of *thirty per cent.* per annum. After various ineffectual trials, Nightingale abandoned all hope of affording the promised succor, and thus Whitney was compelled to forego the great advantages he confidently anticipated from the voyage to England.

We regret that we have not been able to obtain the letters written at this period by Mr. Whitney to his partner, but the nature of their contents will be easily gathered from those of Mr. Miller.

In March, 1797, Mr. Miller says, "Unless Nightingale should have the power to assist you with some supplies, which your letter furnishes little ground to hope, I foresee that our money engagements cannot be complied with ; and we can only regret as a misfortune what we cannot remedy. In the event of this failure, I can only take to myself the one half of the blame which may attach itself to our misplaced confidence in the public opinion. I confess myself to have been entirely deceived in supposing that an *egregious error*, and a general deception with regard to the quality of our cotton, could not long continue to influence the whole of the manufacturing, the mercantile, and the planting interests, against us. But the reverse of this fact, allowing the staple of our cotton to be uninjured, has to our sorrow proved true, and I have long apprehended that our ruin would be the inevitable consequence.

"I am now devoting my time and attention to prepare, in

the best manner in my power, the suits which are to be tried in April ; and am determined that all the dark clouds of adversity, which at present overshadow our affairs, shall not abate my ardor in laboring to burst through them, in order to reach the dawn of prosperity, that has so long been withheld from our view."

Notwithstanding the disastrous condition of the affairs of Miller & Whitney, Mr. Nightingale, who was of an adventurous spirit, having partially extricated himself from his own embarrassments, was ready to purchase a part of their concern, and offered upon certain conditions to advance five thousand dollars to the company.

We have before us a letter written by Mr. Whitney, dated Oct. 7th, 1797, from which it will be seen what was the state of his affairs and of his feelings at this period. " The extreme embarrassments (says he) which have been for a long time accumulating upon me, are now become so great, that it will be impossible for me to struggle against them many days longer. It has required my utmost exertions *to exist*, without making the least progress in our business. I have labored hard against the strong current of disappointment, which has been threatening to carry us down the cataract, but I have labored with a shattered oar and struggled in vain, unless some speedy relief is obtained. I am now quite far enough advanced in life to think seriously of marrying. I have ever looked forward with pleasure to an alliance with an amiable and virtuous companion, as a source from whence I have expected one day to derive the greatest happiness. But the accomplishment of my tour to Europe, and the acquisition of something which I can call my own, appears to be absolutely necessary, before it will be admissable for me even *to think* of family engagements. Probably a year and a half, at least, will be required to perform that tour, after it is entered upon. Life is but short at best, and six or seven years out of the midst of it, is, to him who makes it, an immense sacrifice. My most unremitted attention has been devoted to our business. I have sacrificed to it other objects from which, before this time, I might certainly have gained twenty or thirty thousand dollars. My whole prospects have been embarked in it, with the expectation that I should, before this time, have realized something from it."

These observations are made with reference to a proposition which he had brought forward, to be allowed to retain a certain portion of the proceeds of the receipts from Mr. Nightingale as his private property; or, at least, to be permitted to adopt such arrangements as would secure it to him after a limited period. But the involved state of the company concerns was such that Mr. Miller would not consent to such an arrangement, nor does it appear to have ever been made. However, brighter prospects seemed now to be opening upon them, from the more favorable reports that were made respecting the quality of their cotton. Respectable manufacturers, both at home and abroad, gave favorable certificates, and retailing merchants sought for the cotton cleaned by Whitney's gin, because it was greatly preferred by their customers to any other in the market. This favorable turn in public opinion, would have restored prosperity to the company, had not the encroachments on the patent-right become so extensive as almost to annihilate its value.

The issue of the first trial they were able to obtain, is announced in the following letter from Mr. Miller, dated May 11, 1797.

" The event of the first patent suit, after all our exertions made in such a variety of ways, has gone against us. The preposterous custom of trying civil causes of this intricacy and magnitude, by a common jury, together with the imperfection of the patent law, frustrated all our views, and disappointed expectations, which had become very sanguine. The tide of popular opinion was running in our favor, the Judge was well disposed towards us, and many decided friends were with us, who adhered firmly to our cause and interests. The Judge gave a charge to the jury pointedly in our favor ; after which the defendant himself told an acquaintance of his, that he would give two thousand dollars to be free from the verdict; and yet the jury gave it against us after a consultation of about an hour. And having made the verdict general, no appeal would lie.

" On Monday morning, when the verdict was rendered, we applied for a new trial ; but the Judge refused it to us on the ground that the jury might have made up their opinion on the defect of the law, which makes an aggression consist of *making, devising, and using, or selling :* whereas we could only charge the defendant with *using.*

" Thus after four years of assiduous labor, fatigue and difficulty, are we again set afloat by a new and most unexpected obstacle. Our hopes of success are now removed to a period still more distant than before, while our expenses are realized beyond all controversy."

Great efforts were made to obtain a trial in a second suit, at the session of the court in Savannah, in May, 1798. A great number of witnesses were collected from various parts of the country, to the distance of a hundred miles from Savannah, when, behold, no Judge appeared, and of course no court was held. In consequence of the failure of the first suit, and so great a procrastination of the second, the encroachments on the patent-right had been prodigiously multiplied, so as almost entirely to destroy the business of the patentees.

In April, 1799, Mr. Miller writes as follows. " The prospect of making any thing by ginning in this State, is at an end. Surreptitious gins are erected in every part of the country ; and the jurymen at Augusta have come to an understanding among themselves, that they will never give a verdict in our favor, let the merits of the case be as they may."

The company would now have gladly relinquished the plan of working their own machines, and confined their operations to the sale of patent-rights ; but few would buy a patent-right which they could use with impunity without purchasing, and those few, hardly in a single instance, paid cash, but gave their notes, which they afterwards to a great extent avoided paying, either by obtaining a verdict from the juries declaring them void, or by contriving to postpone the collection until they were barred by the statute of limitations, a period of only four years. When thus barred, the agent of Miller & Whitney, who was dispatched on a collecting tour through the State of Georgia, informed them, that such obstacles were thrown in his way from one or the other of the foregoing causes, he was unable to collect money enough from all these claims to bear his expenses, but was compelled to draw for nearly the whole amount of these upon his employers.

The agent here referred to was Russel Goodrich, Esq., who had engaged in the service of Miller & Whitney, as early as the year 1798. He was educated at Yale College, in the same class with Mr. Miller, and was for many years an able and zealous agent in the affairs, first of the company, and after the decease of Mr. Miller, of Mr. Whitney.

In a letter addressed to Mr. Whitney, dated Georgia, September 3d, 1801, Mr. Goodrich writes thus : " I have spent a part of this summer in South Carolina, upon the business of Miller & Whitney. Many of the planters of that region expressed an opinion, that if an application were made to their legislature by the citizens to purchase the right of the patentees for that State, there was no doubt that it would be done to the satisfaction of all parties. Accordingly, they had petitions circulated among the people, which appeared to be generally approved of, and were very generally signed." Mr. Goodrich further urges the importance of Mr. Whitney's coming on to South Carolina, to attend at the approaching session of the legislature, in order to make the proposed contract.

Accordingly, Mr. Whitney repaired to Columbia, taking the city of Washington in his way, where he was furnished with very obliging letters from President Jefferson and Mr. Madison, then Secretary of State, testimonials which no doubt were of great service to him in his subsequent negotiations. Soon after the opening of the session of the legislature, in the month of Dec., 1801, the business was regularly brought before the legislature, and a joint committee of both Houses appointed to treat with the patentees. To this committee Messrs. Miller & Whitney submitted the following proposals :—

" *To the Joint Committee of both Houses of the Legislature of South Carolina.*
" Gentlemen,

" The subscribers, in estimating the value of their property in the Patent Machine for cleaning cotton, commonly called the Saw Gin, are influenced by the following considerations, viz :

" That no right of property is so well founded in nature, as that of one's own invention; that their fellow citizens by their representatives in the national Government, from considerations both of policy and justice, have declared that individuals who will use their exertions to acquire this species of property, shall enjoy an exclusive right in the same for fourteen years; that influenced by, and relying on, these declarations of their country, they have spent a number of years, and exhausted their funds, in inventing and bringing into use, their Saw Gin ; that notwithstanding the innumerable misrepresentations and prejudices which have gone forth respecting this concern, they have firm reliance on the laws of their country, and feel a conscious rectitude in the justice of their cause.

" When we look around and see many of our fellow citizens, who are engaged in pursuits exclusively for their *own* benefit, guarded and protected in those pursuits by the laws of their country, we cannot believe that those who have contributed, in any degree, to benefit their *fellow citizens* and the public, will be deprived of the same protection, and abandoned to poverty.

" We will not go into any detailed calculations as to the value of this invention, but only observe, that the citizens of South Carolina have gained, and will gain, many millions of dollars by the use of this machine, which they never could have acquired without it. Being under embarrassments in consequence of debts incurred in prosecuting this undertaking, and desirous of obtaining some compensation for our labors, we will not measure our demand by the value of the property, but are willing to dispose of it to the State of South Carolina for a sum far below its real value ; and therefore we submit to the committee the following Proposals :

" The subscribers will relinquish and transfer to the legislature of South Carolina so much of their patent-right of the machine for separating cotton from its seeds, commonly called the Saw Gin, as appertains to said State, for the sum of one hundred thousand dollars, the one half of the said sum to be paid on the transfer of said right, the other by installments, as shall be hereafter agreed upon.   Miller & Whitney."

After some discussion, it was agreed by the legislature to offer to the patentees the sum of *fifty thousand dollars.* We subjoin a letter, addressed at this time by Mr. Whitney to his friend Stebbins, both as a statement of the particulars relating to the contract, and as evincive of the feelings of the writer :

" Columbia, South Carolina, Dec. 20, 1801.
" *Dear Stebbins,*

" I have been at this place a little more than two weeks, attending the legislature. They closed their session at ten o'clock last evening. A few hours previous to their adjournment, they voted to purchase, for the State of South Carolina, my patent-right to the machine for cleaning cotton, at fifty thousand dollars, of which sum, *twenty thousand is to be paid in hand, and the remainder in three annual payments of ten thousand dollars each.*

"This is selling the right at a great sacrifice. If a regular course of law had been pursued, from two to three hundred thousand dollars would undoubtedly have been recovered. The use of the machine here is amazingly extensive, and the value of it beyond all calculation. It may, without exaggeration, be said to have raised the value of seven eights of all the three Southern States from fifty to one hundred per cent. We get but a song for it in comparison with the worth of the thing ; but it is *securing* something. It will enable Miller & Whitney to pay all their debts, and divide something between them. It establishes a precedent which will be valuable as it respects our collections in other States, and I think there is now a fair prospect that I shall in the event realize property enough to render me comfortable, and in some measure independent.

"Though my stay here has been short, I have become acquainted with a considerable part of the members of the legislature, and of the most distinguished characters in the State. My old classmate, H. D. W., is one of the Senate. He ranks among the first of his age in point of talents and respectability. He has shown me much polite attention, as have also many others of the citizens.

Truly your friend,
J. Stebbins, Esq. Eli Whitney."

In December, 1802, Mr. Whitney negotiated a sale of his patent-right with the State of North Carolina. The legislature laid a tax of two shillings and sixpence upon *every saw** employed in ginning cotton, to be continued for five years, which sum was to be collected by the sheriffs in the same manner as the public taxes ; and after deducting the expenses of collection, the avails were faithfully paid over to the patentee. At that time the culture of cotton had made comparatively little progress in the State of North Carolina ; but, in proportion to the amount of interest concerned, this compensation was regarded by Mr. Whitney as more liberal than that received from any other source.

While these encouraging prospects were rising in North Carolina, Mr. Goodrich, the agent of the company, was entering into a similar negotiation with the State of Tennessee. The importance of the machine began to be universally acknowledged in that State, and various public meetings of the citizens were held, in which were adopted resolutions strongly in favor of a public contract with Miller & Whitney.† Accordingly, the legislature of Tennessee, at their session in 1803, passed an act laying a tax of thirty seven cents and a half per annum on every saw, for the period of four years.

But while a fairer day seemed dawning upon the company in this quarter, an unexpected and threatening cloud was rising in another. It was during Mr. Whitney's negotiation with the legislature of North Carolina, that he received intelligence that the legislature of South Carolina had annulled the contract made with Miller & Whitney the preceding year, had suspended payment of the balance (thirty thousand dollars) due them, and instituted a suit for the recovery of what had already been paid to them.

The ostensible causes of this extraordinary measure adopted by the legislature of South Carolina, were a distrust of the validity of the patent-right, and failure on the part of the patentees to perform certain conditions agreed on in the contract.

---

* Some of the gins had forty saws.

† Of one of these meetings, General Jackson, late President of the United States, was chairman.

Great exertions had constantly been made in Georgia to impress the public with the notion, that Mr. Whitney was not the original inventor of the cotton gin, somebody in Switzerland having conceived the idea of it before him, and, especially, that he was not entitled to the credit of the invention in its improved form, in which saws were used instead of wire teeth, inasmuch as this particular form of the machine was introduced by one Hodgin Holmes. It was on these grounds that the Governor of Georgia, in his message to the legislature of that State in 1803, urged the inexpediency of granting any thing to Miller & Whitney. We have before us a copy of the report of the committee appointed on that part of the Governor's message, and since it will serve to show both the grounds and the character of the opposition, we will subjoin a few extracts from it.*

" The Committee to whom was referred, &c. Report :—

" That they have carefully attended to that part of the communication which relates to the Cotton Gin, and cordially agree with the Governor in his observations, that monopolies are at all times odious, particularly in free governments, and that some remedy ought to be applied to the wound which the cotton gin monopoly has given, and will otherwise continue to give, to the culture and cleaning of that precious and increasing staple. They have examined the Rev. James Hutchinson, who declares that Edward Lyon, at least twelve months before Miller & Whitney's machine was brought into view, had in possession a saw or cotton gin, in miniature, of the same construction ; and it further appears to them, from the information of Doctor Cortes Pedro Dampiere, an old and respectable citizen of Columbia County, that a machine of a construction similar to that of Miller & Whitney, was used in Switzerland, at least forty years ago, for the purpose of picking rags to make lint and paper.

" That, however, as Congress has the constitutional power

---

* In adverting to these transactions of former times, it is no part of our purpose to revive unpleasant recollections, or to throw discredit on the history of the very respectable States above named ; but without the recital of these facts, the life of Whitney could not have been written.

to establish patents of the nature of Miller & Whitney's, the commitee, uniting with the Governor in opinion that no legislative power but Congress can interfere, and also convinced that in the passage of the law Congress could have had no idea of laying the two Southern States, and in all probability North Carolina and Tennessee, under contribution to two individuals, (the article at the passing of the first act not being thought of, as about to become the principal staple of export from those States,) do recommend the following resolutions :

"*Resolved*, That the Senators and Representatives of this State in Congress be, and they hereby are, instructed to use their utmost endeavors to obtain a modification of the act, entitled an act to extend the privilege of obtaining Patents for useful discoveries and inventions, to certain persons therein mentioned, and to enlarge and define the penalties for violating the rights of patentees, so as to prevent the operation of it, to the injury of that most valuable staple cotton, and the cramping of genius in improvements, in Miller & Whitney's patent Gin, as well as to limit the price of obtaining a right of using it, the price at present being unbounded, and the planter and poor artificer altogether at the mercy of the patentees, who may raise the price to any sum they please.

" And in case the said Senators and Representatives of this State shall find such modification impracticable, that they do then use their best endeavors to induce Congress, from the example of other nations, to make compensation to Miller & Whitney for their discovery, take up the patent-right, and release the Southern States from so burthensome a grievance.

" *Resolved*, That his Excellency the Governor be requested to transmit copies of the foregoing report and resolutions to the Executives of the States of South Carolina, North Carolina, and Tennessee, to be laid before their respective legislatures, with a request of coöperation, through their Senators and Representatives in Congress."

Popular feeling, stimulated by the most sordid motives, was now awakened throughout all the cotton-growing States. Tennessee followed the example of South Carolina, in suspending the payment of the tax laid upon cotton gins, and a

similar attempt was made at a subsequent session of the legislature of North Carolina ; but it wholly failed, and the report of
a committee, offering a resolution that " the contract ought to
be fulfilled with punctuality and good faith," was adopted by
both branches of the legislature.

There were also high-minded men in South Carolina, who
were indignant at the dishonorable measures adopted by their
legislature of 1803, and their sentiments had impressed the
community so favorably with regard to Mr. Whitney, that at
the session of 1804, the legislature not only rescinded what the
previous legislature had done, but signified their respect for
Mr. Whitney, by marked commendations.

Nor ought it to be forgotten, that there were in Georgia too
those who viewed with scorn and indignation the base
attempts of men, led by unprincipled demagogues, to defraud
Mr. Whitney. The Augusta Herald of January 10, 1805,
mentions the transactions in South Carolina in the following
manner :

" Our readers will no doubt recollect that the legislature of
South Carolina, a year or two past, purchased of Messrs. Miller & Whitney the patent-right of using the Saw Gin in that
State, for the sum of fifty thousand dollars. In this contract,
Mr. Whitney was obligated, within a stipulated time, to furnish the State with two models of the Saw Gin, of the best
size and make, according to his opinion, for separating cotton
from its seed. From some unexpected circumstances the
models were not furnished in due time ; and some gross misrepresentations having been made to a subsequent legislature
of that State, and considerable improper exertion having been
made to persuade them that Mr. Whitney was not the original
inventor of the Saw Gin, they rather precipitately passed an
act for a resolution, suspending the execution of their contract, and directing a suit to be brought against Messrs. Miller
& Whitney for the recovery of twenty thousand dollars,
which, as part of the contract, had been paid them. At the
last session of the legislature, Mr. Whitney was enabled
not only to furnish satisfactory evidence of his being the
original inventor of the gin, but to explain away all former

misrepresentations, and to show that the very patent of the person who had attempted to wrest from him his right, had been repealed in a court of justice. Two models of a gin were also furnished by Mr. Whitney, executed, we are told, in a most superior and masterly manner, and far surpassing in excellence any machinery of the kind ever before seen—they were of metal, and so nicely and substantially made, that it was hardly possible for them to get out of order ; and they worked with such ease, that when the hopper of a forty Saw Gin was filled with cotton, the labor of turning it was not greater than that of turning a common grindstone. The models were highly approved, and the legislature did not hesitate to do justice to the ingenious inventor, according to their original agreement ; and we are pleased to see that they disclaimed the monstrous doctrine of a legislature's having authority to rescind a solemn contract made with an individual, and of their being justified in refusing to do right, because they have the power to do wrong.

" Our sister State of South Carolina has usually been very far from discovering any disposition to do injustice to individuals, and their proceedings against Mr. Whitney were predicated upon imposition practised on them, and their recent conduct evidences that they were satisfied thereof.

" The following is the report of the committee :—

" *The joint Committee of both branches of the legislature, to whom was referred the memorial of Eli Whitney, Report,*

" That on the most mature deliberation, they are of opinion that Miller & Whitney, from whom the State of South Carolina purchased the patent-right for using the Saw Gin within this State, have used due and proper diligence to refund the money and notes received by them from divers citizens ; and as from several unforeseen occurrences the said Miller & Whitney have heretofore been prevented from refunding the same, they therefore recommend that the money and notes aforesaid be deposited with the Comptroller General, to be paid over, on demand, to the several persons from whom the same have been received, upon their delivering up the licenses for which the said notes of hand were given, and said moneys paid to the Comptroller General, and that he be directed to hold the said licenses subject to the order of said Whitney.

" That the excellent and highly improved models now offered by the said Whitney, be received in full satisfaction of the stipulations of the contract between the State and Miller & Whitney, relative to the same ; and that the suit commenced by the State against said Miller & Whitney, be discontinued.

" The joint committee taking every circumstance alledged in the memorial into their serious consideration, further recommend, that (as the good faith of this State is pledged for the payment of the purchase of the said patent-right) the contract be now fulfilled, as in their opinion it ought to be, according to the most strict justice and equity.

" And although from the documents exhibited by said Whitney to the committee, they are of opinion that the said Whitney is the true, original inventor of the Saw Gin, yet in order to guard the citizens from any injury hereafter, the committee recommend, that before the remaining balance is paid, the said Whitney be required to give bond and security to the Comptroller General, to indemnify each and every citizen of South Carolina against the legal claims of all persons whatsoever, other than the said Miller & Whitney, to any patent or exclusive right to the invention or improvement of the machine for separating cotton from its seeds, commonly called the Saw Gin, in the form and upon the principles which it is now and has heretofore been used in this State.

" The preceding report was adopted by both branches of the legislature."

When Mr. Whitney first heard of the transactions of the South Carolina legislature annulling their contract, he was at Raleigh, where he had just concluded his negotiation with the legislature of North Carolina. In a letter written to Mr. Miller at this time he remarks : " I am, for my own part, more vexed than alarmed by their extraordinary proceedings. I think it behooves us to be very cautious and circumspect in our measures and even in our remarks with regard to it. Be cautious what you say or publish till we meet our enemies in a court of justice, when, if they have any sensibility left, we will make them very much ashamed of their childish conduct."

But that Mr. Whitney felt very keenly in regard to the severities afterwards practised towards him, is evident from the tenor of the remonstrance which he presented to the legislature. "The subscriber (says he) respectfully solicits permission to represent to the legislature of South Carolina, that he conceives himself to have been treated with unreasonable severity in the measures recently taken against him by and under their immediate direction. He holds that, to be seized and dragged to prison without being allowed to be heard in answer to the charge alledged against him, and indeed without the exhibition of any specific charge, is a direct violation of the common right of every citizen of a free government; that the power, in this case, is all on one side; that whatever may be the issue of the process now instituted against him, he must, in any case, be subjected to great expense and extreme hardships; and that he considers the tribunal before which he is holden to appear, to be wholly incompetent to decide, definitely, existing disputes between the State and Miller & Whitney.

"The subscriber avers that he has manifested no other than a disposition to fulfill all the stipulations entered into with the State of South Carolina, with punctuality and good faith; and he begs leave to observe farther, that to have industriously, laboriously, and exclusively devoted many years of the prime of his life to the invention and the improvement of a machine, from which the citizens of South Carolina have already realized immense profits,—which is worth to them millions, and from which their posterity, to the latest generations, must continue to derive the most important benefits, and in return to be treated as a felon, a swindler, and a villain, has stung him to the very soul. And when he considers that this cruel persecution is inflicted by the very persons who are enjoying these great benefits, and expressly for the purpose of preventing his ever deriving the least advantage from his own labors, the acuteness of his feelings is altogether inexpressible."

At this time a new and unexpected responsibility devolved on Mr. Whitney, in consequence of the death of his partner,

Mr. Miller, who died on the 7th of December, 1803. Mr.
Miller had, in the early stages of the enterprise, indulged very
high hopes of a sudden fortune; but perpetual disappointments appear to have attended him throughout the remainder
of his life. The history of them, as detailed in his volumin-
ous correspondence, which is now before us, affords an instructive exemplification of the anxiety, toil, and uncertainty,
that frequently accompany too eager a pursuit of wealth, and
the pain and disappointment that follow in the train of expectations too highly elated. If Mr. Miller anticipated a great
bargain from an approaching auction of cotton, some sly adventurer was sure to step in before him, and bid it out of his
hands. If he looked to his extensive rice crops, cultivated on
the estate of General Greene, as the means of raising money
to extricate himself from the numerous embarrassments into
which he had fallen, a severe drought came on and shriveled
the crop, or floods of rain suddenly destroyed it. The markets unexpectedly changed at the very moment of selling, and
always to his disadvantage. Heavy rains likewise destroyed
the cotton crops on which he had counted for thousands; and
more than all, wicked and dishonest men contrived to cheat
him of his just rights; and thus his airy hopes were often frustrated, until at length the speculations in Yazoo lands beguiled
him into inextricable difficulties, and in the midst of all, and
on the dawn of a brighter day, death stepped in and dissolved
the pageant that had so long been dancing before his eyes.

Mr. Whitney was now left alone, to contend singly against
those difficulties which had for a series of years almost broken down the spirits of both the partners. The light, moreover, which seemed to be rising upon them, from the favorable
occurrences of the preceding year, proved but the twilight of
prosperity, and a darker night seemed about to supervene.

But the favorable issue of the affairs of Mr. Whitney in
South Carolina, during the subsequent year, and the generous
receipts that he obtained from the avails of his contracts with
North Carolina, relieved him from the embarrassments under
which he had so long groaned, and made him in some degree
independent. Still, no small portion of the funds thus collect' 1

in North and South Carolina, was expended in carrying on the fruitless, endless lawsuits in Georgia.

In the United States Court, held in Georgia, in December, 1807, Mr. Whitney obtained a most important decision, in a suit brought against a trespasser of the name of Fort. It was on this trial that Judge Johnson gave his celebrated decision. It was in the following words :

> " *Whitney*, survivor of ⎫
> *Miller & Whitney*, ⎬ In equity.
> vs. ⎪
> *Arthur Fort*. ⎭

" The complainants, in this case, are proprietors of the machine called the saw gin. The use of which is to detach the short staple cotton from its seed.

" The defendant, in violation of their patent-right, has constructed, and continues to use this machine ; and the object of this suit is to obtain a perpetual injunction to prevent a continuance of this infraction of complainant's right.

" Defendant admits most of the facts in the bill set forth, but contends that the complainants are not entitled to the benefits of the act of Congress on this subject, because—

1st. The invention is not original.

2d. Is not useful.

3d. That the machine which he uses is materially different from their invention, in the application of an improvement, the invention of another person.

" The court will proceed to make a few remarks upon the several points, as they have been presented to their view: whether the defendant was now at liberty to set up this defence, whilst the patent-right of complainants remains unrepealed, has not been made a question, and they will therefore not consider it.

" To support the originality of the invention, the complainants have produced a variety of depositions of witnesses, examined under commission, whose examination expressly proves the origin, progress, and completion of the machine by Whitney, one of the co-partners. Persons who were made privy to his first discovery, testify to the several experiments which he made in their presence, before he ventured to expose his invention to the scrutiny of the public eye. But it is not necessary to resort to such testimony to maintain this point· The jealousy of the artist to maintain that reputation which his ingenuity has justly acquired, has urged him to unnecessary pains on this subject. There are circumstances in the knowledge of all mankind, which prove the originality of this invention more satisfactorily to the mind, than the direct testimony of a host of witnesses. The cotton plant furnished clothing to mankind before the age of Herodotus. The green seed is a species much more productive than the black, and by nature adapted to a much greater variety of climate. But by reason of the strong adherence of the fibre to the seed, without the aid of some more powerful machine for separating it, than any formerly known among us, the cultivation of it would never have been made an object. The machine of which Mr. Whitney claims the invention, so facilitates the preparation of this species for use, that the cultivation of it has suddenly become an object of infinitely greater national importance than that of the other species ever can be. Is it then to be imagined that if this machine had been before discovered, the use of it would ever have been lost, or could have been confined to any tract or country left unexplored by commercial enterprise ? But it is unnecessary to remark further upon this subject. A number of years have elapsed since Mr. Whitney took out his patent, and no one has produced or pretended to prove the existence of a machine of similar construction or use.

" 2d. With regard to the utility of this discovery, the Court would deem it a waste of time to dwell long upon this topic. Is there a man who hears us, who has not experienced its utility ? The whole interior of the Southern States was languishing, and its inhabitants emigrating for want of some object to engage their attention and employ their industry, when the invention of this machine at once opened views to them, which set the whole country in active motion. From childhood to age it has presented to us a lucrative employment. Individuals who were depressed with poverty and sunk in idleness, have suddenly risen to wealth and respectability. Our debts have been paid off. Our capitals have increased, and our lands trebled themselves in value. We cannot express the weight of the obligation which the country owes to this invention. The extent of it cannot now be seen. Some faint presentiment may be formed from the reflection that cotton is rapidly supplanting wool, flax, silk, and even furs in manufactures, and may one day profitably supply the use of specie in our East India trade. Our sister States, also, participate in the benefits of this invention; for, besides affording the raw material for their manufacturers, the bulkiness and quantity of the article afford a valuable employment for their shipping.

"3d. The third and last ground taken by defendant, appears to be that on which he mostly relies. In the specification, the teeth made use of are of strong wire inserted into the cylinder. A Mr. Holmes has cut teeth in plates of iron, and passed them over the cylinder. This is certainly a meritorious improvement in the mechanical process of constructing this machine. But at last, what does it amount to, except a more convenient mode of making the same thing? Every characteristic of Mr. Whitney's machine is preserved. The cylinder, the iron tooth, the rotary motion of the tooth, the breast work and brush, and all the merit that this discovery can assume, is that of a more expeditious mode of attaching the tooth to the cylinder. After being attached, in operation and effect they are entirely the same. Mr. Whitney may not be at liberty to use Mr. Holmes' iron plate, but certainly Mr. Holmes' improvement does not destroy Mr. Whitney's patent-right. Let the decree for a perpetual injunction be entered."

This favorable decision, however, did not put a final stop to aggression. At the next session of the United States Court, two other actions were brought, and verdicts for damages gained of two thousand dollars in one case, and one thousand five hundred dollars in the other. The history of these suits, as reported for one of the journals of the day, appears to us to be a document worth preserving, on account of the light it throws on the subject of patent-rights in general, as well as in relation to the subject before us.

LAW CASE.—At a Circuit Court of the United States, for the district of Georgia, lately holden in this city, [Savannah,] was tried the case of Eli Whitney *vs.* Isaiah Carter, for infringing a right vested by patent, " for a new and useful improvement in the mode of ginning cotton." The plaintiff supported his declaration by proving the patent, model, and specification, and proving the use of the machine in question by the defendant. He also introduced the testimony of several witnesses residing in New Haven, to prove the origin and progress of his invention.

The defendant rested his defence on two grounds—First : That the machine was not originally invented by Whitney.— Second : That the specification does not contain the whole truth, relative to the discovery.

General Mitchell, of counsel for the defendant, produced a model which was intended to represent a machine used in Great Britain for cleaning cotton, denominated the " *Teazer or Devil.*"—A witness was produced, who testified that he had seen in England, about seventeen years ago, a machine for separating cotton from the seed, which resembled in principle the model now exhibited by defendant.

Another witness testified, that he had seen a machine in Ireland, upon the same principle, which was used for separating the motes from the cotton before going to the carding machine.

By the machine, of which a model was exhibited, the cotton is applied in the first instance to rollers made of iron, revolving conversely. By these rollers, the fibres are separated from the seeds and protruded within the sweep of certain straight pieces of wire, revolving on a cylinder, which tear and loosen the cotton as they revolve. It was contended by the defendant's counsel, that this model conforms in principle to Mr. Whitney's machine, and that the evidence given in support of it, establishes a presumption, that he must have derived the plan of his machine from a similar one used in the cotton manufactories in Great Britain.

In support of the second ground of defence, evidence was produced to show that Mr. Whitney now uses, and that the defendant also uses, teeth formed of circular iron plates, instead of teeth made of wire. And it was contended that this is a departure from the specification, and an improvement on the original discovery, which destroys the merit of that discovery, and the validity of plaintiff's patent. It was also insisted that the plaintiff had concealed the best means of producing the effect contemplated.

Mr. Noel, of counsel for the plaintiff, in opposition to the first ground of defence, stated two points—First : That if the principle be the same, yet the plaintiff's application of that principle being new, and for a distinct purpose, has all the merit of an original invention.   Second : That the principle of Mr. Whitney's machine is entirely different from that exhibited by defendant.

He defined the term principle, as applied to mechanic arts, to mean the elements and rudiments of those arts, or, in other words, the first ground and rule for them : that for a mere principle, a patent cannot be obtained : that neither the elements, nor the manner of combining them, nor even the effect produced, can be the subject of a patent, and that it can only be obtained for the application of this effect to some new and useful purpose.

To prove this position, several examples were stated of important inventions, for which patents had been obtained, which had resulted from principles previously in common use, and an argument of a celebrated Judge, at Westminster Hall, was cited, in which it was asserted, "that two thirds or three fourths of all patents granted since the statute passed, are for methods of operating and manufacturing, producing no new substances, and employing no new machinery ;" and he adds, in the significant words of Lord Mansfield, " a patent must be for method, detached from all physical existence whatever."

The second point was principally relied on, to wit : That the principle of Mr. Whitney's machine is distinct from that produced by defendant, and new in its origin.

It consists of teeth, or sharp metallic points, of a particular form and shape, and its application is to separate cotton from the seed ; whereas the principle of the model exhibited by the defendant, and of every other machine before invented, and used for the same, or any similar purpose, consists of two small rollers made of wood or iron. In illustration of this point, the plaintiff's counsel cited the opinion of this court, delivered by Judge Johnson, in December term, 1807, in the case of Whitney and others *vs.* Fort, upon a bill for injunction.

The second objection relied on by the defendant, was " that the specification does not contain the whole truth respecting the discovery." To this it was answered, that by the testimony it appears Mr. Whitney, in the original construction of his machine, contemplated each mode of making the teeth, and doubted which mode was best adapted to the purpose. If the alteration which forms the basis of this objection has the merit of an improvement, how far does it extend? An improvement, not in the principle, nor in the operation of the machine, but in making one of its component parts; merely in forming the same thing, to produce the same effect, by means somewhat different. In the case above cited, Judge Johnson remarked on this point, as follows:

" A Mr. Holmes has cut teeth in plates of iron, and passed them over the cylinder. This is certainly a meritorious improvement in the mechanical process of constructing this machine. But at last, what does it amount to, except a more convenient mode of making the same thing? Every characteristic of Mr. Whitney's machine is preserved. The cylinder, the iron tooth, rotary motion of the tooth, the breast work and brush, and all the merit that this discovery can assume, is that of a more expeditious mode of attaching the tooth to the cylinder."

The counsel for Whitney admitted that an improvement in a particular part of the machine would entitle the inventor to a patent for a new and better mode of making that specific part, but not for the whole machine, as in the case of Boulton *vs.* Bull, where a patent was granted for an invention to lessen the quantity of fuel in the use of a certain Steam Engine. It was decided " that the patent was valid for this improvement, but that it gave no title to the engine itself."

It was also stated, that by experiments made on plaintiff's

model in the face of the court and jury, and by testimony produced, it was apparent no improvement had resulted from this alteration; that no beneficial change or amendment in the principle had taken place; nor had the effect been aided or facilitated. In the charge of the court to the jury, Judge Stephens remarked, that the case cited, *Whitney and others vs. Fort*, was decided without any evidence on the part of the defendant:—that from the testimony now produced, his opinion is, that the plaintiff must have received his first impressions from a machine previously in use, on a similar principle; and that an improvement had been made as to the teeth, by which the merit of Mr. Whitney's original invention was diminished. For these reasons Judge Stephens had some doubts whether the plaintiff ought to recover.

Judge Johnson remarked to the jury, that after hearing the evidence which had been relied on by the defendant, he remained content with the opinion which he had given in the case of Whitney against Fort, and that he was also as fully satisfied with the charge he was about to give, as any he had delivered. That as to the origin of this invention, the plaintiff's title remained unimpeached by any evidence which has been adduced in this cause. He agreed with the plaintiff's counsel, that the legal title to a patent consists not in a principle merely, but in an application of a principle, whether previously in existence or not, to some new and useful purpose. And he was also of opinion, that the principle of Mr. Whitney's machine was entirely new, that it originated with himself, and that it had no resemblance to that of the model exhibited by the defendant.

He considered the defendant's second objection equally unsupported, and referred to the sixth section of the Patent Law of the United States, by which it is required that the concealment alledged (in order to defeat the patentee's recovery) must appear to have been made for the purpose of deceiving the public. That Mr. Whitney, in the original formation of this machine, could have no motive for such concealment, and that in making use of wire, in preference to the other mode, he appears to have acted according to the dictates of his judgment.

If in this instance he erred, the error related to a point not affecting the merit of his invention, or the validity of his patent. Verdict for plaintiff—damages two thousand dollars.

Same Term, Whitney against Gachet, same cause of action. Verdict for plaintiff—damages one thousand five hundred dollars.

The influence of these decisions, however, availed Mr. Whitney very little, for now the term of his patent-right was nearly expired. More than sixty suits had been instituted in Georgia before a single decision on the *merits* of his claim was obtained, and at the period of this decision, thirteen years of his patent had expired. In prosecution of this troublesome business, Mr. Whitney had made six different journeys to Georgia, several of which were accomplished by land, at a time when, compared with the present, the difficulties of such journeys were exceedingly great, and exposed him to excessive fatigues and privations, which at times seriously affected his health, and even jeopardized his life. A gentleman* of much experience in the profession of law, who was well acquainted with Mr. Whitney's affairs in the South, and sometimes acted as his legal adviser, observes, in a letter obligingly communicated to the writer of this memoir, that " in all his experience in the thorny profession of the law, he has never seen such a case of perseverance, under such persecution ; nor (he adds) do I believe that I ever knew any other man who would have met them with equal coolness and firmness, or who would finally have obtained even the partial success which he had. He always called on me in New York, on his way South, when going to attend his endless trials, and to meet the mischievous contrivances of men who seemed inexhaustible in their resources of evil. Even now, after thirty years, my head aches to recollect his narratives of new trials, fresh disappointments, and accumulated wrongs."

We have thought the Cotton Gin sufficiently instructive in its history, and important in its consequences, to merit the attention we have bestowed upon it. After a more cursory

---

* Hon. S. M. Hopkins.

notice of the other chief enterprise which occupied the life of Mr. Whitney, we shall hasten to the conclusion of this memoir.

In 1798, Mr. Whitney became deeply impressed with the uncertainty of all his hopes founded upon the Cotton Gin, notwithstanding their high promise, and he began to think seriously of devoting himself to some business in which superior ingenuity, seconded by uncommon industry, qualifications which he must have been conscious of possessing in no ordinary degree, would conduct him by a slow, but sure route, to a competent fortune ; and we have always considered it indicative of a solid judgment and a well balanced mind, that he did not, as is frequently the case with men of inventive genius, become so poisoned with the hopes of vast and sudden wealth, as to be disqualified for making a reasonable provision for life, by the sober earnings of frugal industry.

The enterprise which he selected in accordance with these views, was the *Manufacture of Arms for the United States.* He accordingly addressed a letter to the Hon. Oliver Wolcott, Secretary of the Treasury, and through his influence obtained a contract for ten thousand stand of arms, amounting (as the price of each musket was to be thirteen dollars and forty cents) to *one hundred and thirty four thousand dollars,*—an undertaking of great responsibility, considering the limited pecuniary resources of the undertaker. This contract was concluded on the 14th of January, 1798, and four thousand were to be delivered on or before the last day of September of the ensuing year, and the remaining six thousand in one year from that time ; so that the whole contract was to be fulfilled within a little more than the period of two years ; and for the due fulfillment of it, Mr. Whitney entered into bonds to the amount of thirty thousand dollars. He must have engaged in this undertaking resolved " to attempt great things," without stopping to weigh all the chances against him ; for as yet, the works were all to be erected, the machinery to be made, and much of it to be invented ; the raw materials were to be collected from different quarters, and the workmen themselves, almost without exception, were yet to learn the trade. Nor was it a business with which Mr. Whitney himself was

particularly conversant. Mechanical invention, a sound judgment, and persevering industry, were all that he possessed, at
first, for the accomplishment of a manufacturing enterprise,
which was at that time probably greater than any man had
ever undertaken, in the State of Connecticut.

The low state of the mechanic arts, moreover, increased
his difficulties. There were in operation near him no kindred
mechanical establishments, upon which some branches of his
own business might lean : even his very tools required to be
to a great extent fabricated by himself. If it is recollected
also, in what a depressed state the cotton ginning business was
at this period, it will appear still more evincive of the bold
spirit of enterprise which Mr. Whitney possessed, as it will be
seen that he could not avail himself of any resources from
that quarter, nor could he reasonably hope to derive from the
same source any future succor. But Mr. Whitney had strong
friends among the most substantial citizens of New Haven,
who had been witnesses alike of the fertility of his genius
and the extent of his industry. Ten of these came forward
as his security to the bank of New Haven, for a loan of ten
thousand dollars. Mr. Wolcott, on the part of the United
States, advanced five thousand more at the time of contract,
with the promise of a similar sum, as soon as the preparatory
arrangements for the manufacture of arms was completed.
No farther advances were to be demanded, until one thousand
stand of arms were ready for delivery; at which time the additional sum of five thousand dollars was to be advanced. Full
payment was to be made on the delivery of each successive
thousand, with occasional advances at the discretion of the
Secretary.

The expenses incurred in getting the establishment fully into
operation, must have greatly exceeded the expectation of the
parties, for advances of ten and fifteen thousand dollars were
successively made by the government, above what was originally contemplated ; but the confidence of the government
seems never to have been impaired ; for the Secretary, after
having examined Mr. Whitney's works in person, declared to
him, in the presence of witnesses, that the advances which he

had made had been laid out with great prudence and economy, and that the undertaker had done more than he should have supposed possible with the sum advanced.

The site which Mr. Whitney had purchased for his works, was at the foot of the celebrated precipice called East Rock, within two miles of New Haven. This spot (which is now called Whitneyville) is justly admired for the romantic beauty of its scenery. A waterfall of moderate extent afforded here the necessary power for propelling the machinery. In this pleasant retreat Mr. Whitney commenced his operations, with the greatest zeal ; but he soon became sensible of the multiplied difficulties which he had to contend with. A winter of uncommon severity set in early and suspended his labors, and when the spring returned, he found himself so little advanced, that he foresaw that he should be utterly unable to deliver the four thousand muskets according to contract. In this predicament, he resolved to throw himself on the indulgence of the enlightened Secretary of the Treasury, to whom he explained at length the various causes which had conspired to retard his operations.

" I find, (says he,) that my personal attention and oversight are more constantly and essentially necessary to every branch of the work, than I apprehended. Mankind, generally, are not to be depended on, and the best workmen I can find are incapable of directing. Indeed, there is no branch of the work that can proceed well, scarcely for a single hour, unless I am present."

At the end of the first year after the contract was made, instead of four thousand muskets, only five hundred were delivered, and it was eight years, instead of two, before the whole ten thousand were completed. The entire business relating to the contract was not closed until January, 1809, when, (so liberally had the government made advances to the contractor,) the final balance due Mr. Whitney was only two thousand four hundred and fifty dollars.

During the ten years Mr. Whitney was occupied in performing this engagement, he applied himself to business with the most exemplary diligence, rising every morning as soon as it was day, and at night, setting every thing in order appertaining to all parts of the establishment, before he retired to rest. His genius impressed itself on every part of the manufactory, extending even to the most common tools, all of which received some peculiar modification which improved them in accuracy, or efficacy, or beauty. His machinery for making the several parts of a musket, was made to operate with the greatest possible degree of uniformity and precision. The object at which he aimed, and which he fully accomplished, was to make the same part of different guns, as the locks, for example, as much like each other as the successive impressions of a copper-plate engraving. It has generally been conceded that Mr. Whitney greatly improved the art of manufacturing arms, and laid his country under permanent obligations, by augmenting her facilities for national defence. So rapid has been the improvement in the arts and manufactures in this country, that it is difficult to conceive of the low state in which they were thirty years ago. To this advancement, the genius and industry of Mr. Whitney most essentially contributed, for while he was clearing off the numerous impediments which were thrown in his way, he was at the same time performing the office of a pioneer to the succeeding generation.

In the year 1812, he entered into a new contract with the United States, to manufacture for them fifteen thousand stand of arms; and in the meantime he executed a similar engagement, (we know not how extensive,) for the State of New York. Although his resources enabled him now to proceed with much greater dispatch, and with far less embarrassment than in his first enterprise, yet some misunderstanding arose with one of the agents of the government, which made it necessary for him to bring his case before the Secretary of War. The following testimonials, which he obtained on this occasion from Governor Tompkins, and from Governor Wolcott, will serve to show in what estimation he was held by those who knew him best, and who were most competent to judge of his merits. The letters, dated May, 1814, are both addressed to General Armstrong, the existing Secretary of War. Governor Tompkins observes as follows : " I have visited Mr. Whitney's establishment at New Haven, and have no hesitation in saying, that I consider it the most perfect I have ever seen; and I believe it is well understood, that few persons in this country surpass Mr. Whitney in talents as a mechanic, or in experience as a manufacturer of muskets. Those which he has made for us, are generally supposed to exceed, in form and quality, all the muskets either of foreign or domestic fabrication, belonging to the State, and are universally preferred and selected by the most competent judges.

" It is perhaps proper for me to observe further, that all Mr. Whitney's contracts with the State of New York have been performed with integrity, and to the entire satisfaction of the several military commissaries of the State."

Governor Wolcott's testimony is still more full, as his opportunities for acquaintance with Mr. Whitney had been more extensive. We insert the letter entire, as not only indicating the high reputation of the individual to whom it relates, but as exemplifying the liberality with which the writer is known always to have fostered and encouraged genius and merit.

" New York, May 7, 1814.

" *Sir*—I have the honor to address you on behalf of my friend, Eli Whitney, Esq., of New Haven, who is a manufacturer of arms, under a contract with your department. Mr. Whitney first engaged in this business under a contract with me, as Secretary of the Treasury; when, according to existing laws, all contracts for military supplies were formed under my superintendence. I have since been constantly acquainted with him, and venture to assure you that the present improved state of our manufactures is greatly indebted to his skill and exertions; that though a practical mechanic, he is also a gentleman of liberal education, a man of science, industry and integrity, and that his inventions and labors have been as useful to this country as those of any other individual. Moreover, that if any further alterations or improvements in the construction of military machines are proposed, Mr. Whitney is one of the few men who can safely and advantageously be consulted, respecting the best mode of giving them effect.

" I make these declarations to you with a perfect conviction that they express nothing more than Mr. Whitney has a

right to demand from every man who is acquainted with his
merits and capable of estimating their value ; and understanding that he experiences some difficulties in regard to his contract, I venture respectfully to request that you would so far
extend to him your favor as to inform yourself particularly of
the merits of his case and the services he can perform ; in
which case I am certain he will receive all the patronage and
protection to which he is entitled.

"I have the honor to remain, with the highest respect, Sir,
your obedient servant, (Signed) OLIVER WOLCOTT.

" *The Hon. Secretary Armstrong.*"

*Several other persons made contracts with the government
at about the same time, and attempted the manufacture of
muskets, following substantially, so far as they understood it,
the method pursued in England. The result of their efforts
was a complete failure to manufacture muskets of the quality
required, at the price agreed to be paid by the government ;
and in some instances they expended in the execution of their
contracts, a considerable fortune in addition to the whole
amount received for their work.

The low state to which the arts had been depressed in this
country by the policy of England, under the colonial system,
and from which they had then scarcely begun to recover, together with the high price of labor and other causes, conspired to render it impracticable at that time even for those
most competent to the undertaking, to manufacture muskets
here in the English method. And doubtless Mr. Whitney
would have shared the fate of his enterprising, but unsuccess-
ful competitors, had he adopted the course which they pursued ; but his genius struck out for him a course entirely new.

In maturing his system he had many obstacles to combat,
and a much longer time was occupied than he had anticipated ;
but with his characteristic firmness he pursued his object, in
the face of the obloquy and ridicule of his competitors, the
evil predictions of his enemies, and the still more discoura-

---

* For the following remarks on the manufacture of arms, the writer of this article is indebted to a gentleman who is personally and intimately acquainted with the
subject.

ging and disheartening misgivings, doubts and apprehensions of his friends. His efforts were at length crowned with success, and he had the satisfaction of finding that the business which had proved so ruinous to others, was likely to prove not altogether unprofitable to himself.

Our limits do not permit us to give a minute and detailed account of this system ; and we shall only glance at two or three of its more prominent features, for the purpose of illustrating its general character.

The several parts of the musket were, under this system, carried along through the various processes of manufacture, in lots of some hundreds or thousands of each. In their various stages of progress, they were made to undergo successive operations by machinery, which not only vastly abridged the labor, but at the same time so fixed and determined their form and dimensions, as to make comparatively little skill necessary in the manual operations. Such were the construction and arrangement of this machinery, that it could be worked by persons of little or no experience, and yet it performed the work with so much precision, that when, in the later stages of the process, the several parts of the musket came to be put together, they were as readily adapted to each other, as if each had been made for its respective fellow. A lot of these parts passed through the hands of several different workmen successively, (and in some cases several times returned, at intervals more or less remote, to the hands of the same workman,) each performing upon them every time some single and simple operation, by machinery or by hand, until they were completed. Thus Mr. Whitney reduced a complex business, embracing many ramifications, almost to a mere succession of simple processes, and was thereby enabled to make a division of the labor among his workmen, on a principle which was not only more extensive, but also altogether more philosophical than that pursued in the English method. In England, the labor of making a musket was divided by making the different workmen the manufacturers of different limbs, while in Mr. Whitney's system the work was divided with reference to its nature, and several workmen performed different operations on the same limb.

It will be readily seen that under such an arrangement any person of ordinary capacity would soon acquire sufficient dexterity to perform a branch of the work. Indeed, so easy did Mr. Whitney find it to instruct new and inexperienced workmen, that he uniformly preferred to do so, rather than to attempt to combat the prejudices of those who had learned the business under a different system.

When Mr. Whitney's mode of conducting the business was brought into successful operation, and the utility of his machinery was fully demonstrated, the clouds of prejudice which lowered over his first efforts were soon dissipated, and he had the satisfaction of seeing not only his system, but most of his machinery, introduced into every other considerable establishment for the manufacture of arms, both public and private, in the United States.

The labors of Mr. Whitney in the manufacture of arms have been often and fully admitted by the officers of the government, to have been of the greatest value to the public interest. A former Secretary of War admitted, in a conversation with Mr. Whitney, that the government were saving twenty five thousand dollars per annum at the two public armories alone, by his improvements. This admission, though it is believed to be far below the truth, is sufficient to show that the subject of this memoir deserved well of his country in this department of her service.

It should be remarked that the utility of Mr. Whitney's labors during the period of his life which we have now been contemplating, was not limited to the particular business in which he was engaged. Many of the inventions which he made to facilitate the manufacture of muskets, were applicable to most other manufactures of iron and steel. To many of these they were soon extended, and became the nucleus around which other inventions clustered ; and at the present time some of them may be recognized in almost every considerable workshop of that description in the United States.

In the year 1812, Mr. W. made application to Congress for

the renewal of his patent for the cotton gin. In his memorial he presented a history of the struggles he had been forced to encounter in defence of his right, observing that he had been unable to obtain any decision on the merits of his claim until he had been *eleven years* in the law, and *thirteen years* of his patent term had expired. He sets forth, that his invention had been a source of opulence to thousands of citizens of the United States ; that as a labor-saving machine it would enable one man to perform the work of a thousand men ; and that it furnishes to the whole family of mankind, at a very cheap rate, the most essential article of their clothing. Hence, he humbly conceived himself entitled to a further remuneration from his country, and thought he ought to be admitted to a more liberal participation with his fellow citizens in the benefits of his invention. Although so great advantages had been already experienced, and the prospect of future benefits was so promising, still many of those whose interest had been most promoted, and the value of whose property had been most enhanced by this invention, had obstinately persisted in refusing to make any compensation to the inventor. The very men whose wealth had been acquired by the use of this machine, and who had grown rich beyond all former example, had combined their exertions to prevent the patentee from deriving any emolument from his invention. From that State in which he had first made and where he had first introduced his machine, and which had derived the most signal benefits from it, he had received nothing ; and from no State had he received the amount of *half a cent per pound* on the cotton cleaned with his machines in one year. Estimating the value of the labor of one man at twenty cents per day, the whole amount which had been received by him for his invention, was not equal to the value of the labor saved *in one hour* by his machines then in use in the United States. " This invention (he proceeds) now gives to the southern section of the Union, over and above the profits which would be derived from the cultivation of any other crop, an annual emolument of at least *three millions* of dollars."* The foregoing statement does not

---

* This was in 1812 ; the amount of profit is at this time incomparably greater.

56

rest on conjecture,—it is no visionary speculation,—all these advantages have been realized; the planters of the southern States have counted the cash, felt the weight of it in their pockets, and heard the exhilarating sound of its collision. Nor do the advantages stop here; this immense source of wealth is but just beginning to be opened. Cotton is a more cleanly and healthful article of cultivation than tobacco and indigo, which it has superseded, and does not so much impoverish the soil. This invention has already trebled the value of the land through a great extent of territory; and the degree to which the cultivation of cotton may be still augmented, is altogether incalculable. This species of cotton has been known in all countries where cotton has been raised, from time immemorial, but was never known as an article of commerce, until since this method of cleaning it was discovered. In short, (to quote the language of Judge Johnson,) if we should assert that the benefits of this invention exceed *one hundred millions of dollars*, we can prove the assertion by correct calculation. It is objected that if the patentee succeeds in procuring the renewal of his patent, he will be too rich. There is no probability that the patentee, if the term of his patent were extended for twenty years, would ever obtain for his invention one half as much as many an individual will gain by the use of it. Up to the present time, the whole amount of what he has acquired from this source, (after deducting his expenses,) does not exceed one half the sum which a single individual has gained by the use of the machine in one year. It is true that considerable sums have been obtained from some of the States where the machine is used; but no small portion of these sums has been expended in prosecuting his claim in a State where nothing has been obtained, and where his machine has been used to the greatest advantage.

" Your memorialist has not been able to discover any reason why he, as well as others, is not entitled to share the benefits of his own labors. He who speculates upon the markets, and takes advantage of the necessities of others, and by these means accumulates property, is called 'a man of enterprise'—'a man of business'—he is complimented for his talents, and is protected by the laws. He, however, only gets into his possession that which was before in the possession of another; he adds nothing to the public stock; and can he who has given thousands to others, be thought unreasonable if he asks one in return?

"It is to be remembered that the pursuit of wealth, by means of new inventions, is a very precarious and uncertain one ;—a lottery where there are many thousand blanks to one prize. Of all the various attempts at improvements, there is probably not more than one in five hundred for which a patent is taken out; and of all the patents taken out, not one in twenty has yielded a net profit to the patentee equal to the amount of the patent fees. In cases where a useful and valuable invention is brought into operation, the reward ought to be in proportion to the hazard of the pursuit. The patent law has now been in operation more than fourteen years. Many suits for damages have been instituted against those who have infringed the right of patentees ; and it is a fact, that very rarely has the patentee ever recovered. If you would hold out inducements for men of *real talents* to engage in these pursuits, your rewards must be sure and substantial. Men of this description can calculate and will know how to appreciate the recompense which they are to receive for their labors. If the encouragement held out be specious and delusive, the discerning will discover the fallacy and will despise it; the weak and visionary only will be decoyed by it, and your patent office will be filled with rubbish. The number of those who succeed in bringing into operation really useful and important improvements, always has been, and always must be, very small. It is not probable that this number can ever be as great as one in a hundred thousand. It is therefore impossible that they can ever exert upon the community an undue influence. There is, on the contrary, much probability and danger that their rights will be trampled on by the many."

Notwithstanding these cogent arguments, the application was rejected by Congress. Some liberal-minded and enlightened men from the cotton districts, favored the petition ; but a majority of the members from that section of the Union were warmly opposed to granting it.

In a correspondence with the late Mr. Robert Fulton, on the same subject, Mr. Whitney observes as follows: " The difficulties with which I have had to contend have originated, principally, in the want of a disposition in mankind to do justice. My invention was new and distinct from every other : it stood alone. It was not interwoven with any thing before known ; and it can seldom happen that an invention or improvement is so strongly marked, and can be so clearly and specifically identified; and I have always believed, that I should have had no difficulty in causing my rights to be respected, if it had been less valuable, and been used only by a small portion of the community. But the use of this machine being immensely profitable to almost every planter in the cotton districts, all were interested in trespassing upon the patent-right, and each kept the other in countenance. Demagogues made themselves popular by misrepresentation and unfounded clamors, both against the right and against the law made for its protection. Hence there arose associations and combinations to oppose both. At one time, but few men in Georgia dared to come into court and testify to the most simple facts within their knowledge, relative to the use of the machine. In one instance, I had great difficulty in proving that the machine *had been used in Georgia*, although, at the same moment, there were three separate sets of this machinery in motion, within fifty yards of the building in which the court sat, and all so near that the rattling of the wheels was distinctly heard on the steps of the court-house."*

---

* In one of his trials, Mr. Whitney adopted the following plan, in order to show how nugatory were the methods of evasion practised by his adversaries. They were endeavoring to have his claim to the invention set aside, on the ground that the teeth in his machine were made of *wire*, inserted into the cylinder of wood, while in the machine of Holmes, the teeth were *cut in plates*, or iron surrounding the cylinder, forming a circular saw. Mr. Whitney, by an ingenious device, (consisting chiefly of sinking the plate below the surface of the cylinder, and suffering the teeth to project,) contrived to give to the saw teeth the appearance of *wires*, while he prepared another cylinder in which the wire teeth were made to look like *saw teeth*. The two cylinders were produced in court, and the witnesses were called on to testify which was the invention of Whitney, and which that of Holmes. They accordingly swore the saw teeth upon Whitney, and the wire teeth upon Holmes ; upon which the Judge declared that it was unnecessary to proceed any farther, the principle of both being manifestly the same.

In the midst of these fruitless efforts to secure to himself some portion of the advantages, which so many of his fellow citizens were reaping from his ingenuity, his armory proceeded with sure but steady pace, which bore him on to affluence. For the few following years he occupied himself principally in the concerns of his manufactory, inventing new kinds of machinery, and improving and perfecting the old.

In January, 1817, Mr. Whitney was married to Miss Henrietta F. Edwards, youngest daughter of the Hon. Pierpont Edwards, late Judge of the District Court for the State of Connecticut. The fond and quiet scenes of domestic life, after which he had so long aspired, but from which he had been debarred by the embarrassed or unsettled state of his affairs, now spread before him in the fairest light. Four children, a son and three daughters,* added successively fresh attractions to the family circle. Happy in his home and easy in his fortune, with a measure of respectability among his fellow citizens, and celebrity abroad, which might well satisfy an honorable ambition, he seemed to have in prospect, after a day of anxiety and toil, an evening unusually bright and serene.

In this uniform and happy tenor, he passed the five following years, when a formidable malady† began to make its approaches, by a slow but hopeless progress, which at length terminated his life.

We are indebted to a near friend and eye witness, for the following account of his last illness. In September, 1822, immediately after his return from Washington, he experienced the first attack of his complaint, which immediately threatened his life. For three weeks the event was very doubtful, during which time he occasionally suffered paroxysms of pain, of from thirty to forty minutes continuance, severe beyond description. These were repeated six or eight times in every twenty four hours. For six weeks he was confined to his

---

* The youngest of these died in September, 1823, aged one year and nine months. Two daughters, and a son bearing his father's name, (the youngest of the three,) still survive.

† An enlargement of the *prostate gland.*

room, at the end of which time he was able to walk about the house, and to enjoy the society of his friends. Early in January, 1823, he had to endure another period of suffering, not less alarming or distressing than the former. With such alternations of awful suffering and partial repose, he reached the 12th of November, 1824, at which period his sufferings became almost unremitted until the 8th of January, 1825, when he expired,—retaining his consciousness to the last, closing his own eyes, and making an effort to close his mouth.

It was his particular request that there should be no examination of his body with a view of ascertaining the nature of his disease, and he desired his funeral to be conducted with as little parade as possible.

The strongest demonstrations of respect and regard were manifested by the citizens of New Haven, in committing his remains to the earth, and the Rev. President Day pronounced over his grave the following eulogy.

" How frequent and how striking are the monitions to us, that this world is not the place of our rest ! It is not often the case, that a man has laid his plans for the business and the enjoyment of life, with a deeper sagacity, than the friend whose remains we have now committed to the dust. He had received, as the gift of heaven, a mind of a superior order. Early habits of thinking gave to it a character of independence and originality. He was accustomed to form his decisions, not after the model of common opinion, but by his own nicely balanced judgment. His mind was enriched with the treasures which are furnished by a liberal education. He had a rare fertility of invention in the arts ; an exactness of execution almost unequalled. By a single exercise of his powers, he changed the state of cultivation, and multiplied the wealth of a large portion of our country. He set an example of system and precision in mechanical operations, which others had not thought of even attempting.

" The high qualities of his mind, instead of unfitting him for ordinary duties, were finely tempered with taste and judgment in the business of life. His manners were formed by an extensive intercourse with the best society. He had an energy of character, which carried him through difficulties, too formidable for ordinary minds.

"With these advantages, he entered on the career of life. His efforts were crowned with success. An ample competency was the reward of his industry and skill. He had gained the respect of all classes of the community. His opinions were regarded with peculiar deference, by the man of science, as well as the practical artist. His large and liberal views, his knowledge of the world, the wide range of his observations, his public spirit, and his acts of beneficence, had given him a commanding influence in society. The gentleness and refinement of his manners, and the delicacy of his feelings in the social and domestic relations, had endeared him to a numerous circle of relatives and friends.

"And what were his reflections in review of the whole, in connection with the distressing scenes of the last period of life? 'All is as the flower of the grass: the wind passeth over it, and it is gone.' All on earth is transient; all in eternity is substantial and enduring. His language was, 'I am a sinner. But God is merciful. The only ground of acceptance before Him, is through the great Mediator.' From this mercy, through this Mediator, is derived our solace under this heavy bereavement. On this, rest the hopes of the mourners, that they shall meet the deceased with joy, at the resurrection of the just."

In his person, Mr. Whitney was considerably above the ordinary size, of a dignified carriage, and of an open, manly, and agreeable countenance. His manners were conciliatory, and his whole appearance such as to inspire universal respect. Among his particular friends, no man was more esteemed. Some of the earliest of his intimate associates were also among the latest. With one or two of the bosom friends of his youth he kept up a correspondence by letter for thirty years, with marks of continually increasing regard. His sense of honor was high, and his feelings of resentment and indignation occasionally strong. He could, however, be cool when his opponents were heated; and, though sometimes surprised by passion, yet the unparalleled trials of patience which he had sustained did not render him petulant, nor did his strong sense of the injuries he had suffered in relation to the cotton gin impair the natural serenity of his temper.

But the most remarkable trait in the character of Mr. Whitney, aside from his inventive powers, was his *perseverance;* and this is the more remarkable, because it is so common to find men of great powers of mechanical invention deficient in this quality. Nothing is more frequent than to see a man of the most fertile powers of invention, run from one piece of mechanism to another, leaving the former half finished ; or if he has completed any thing, it is usual to find him abandon it to others, too fickle to pursue the advantages he might reap from it, or too sensitive to struggle with the sordid and avaricious, who may seek to rob him of the profits of his invention. We cannot better express our views on this subject, than by transcribing from a letter now before us the following remarks communicated to us by a gentleman* who had intimately known Mr. W. from early life.

" I have reflected often and much upon Mr. Whitney's character, and it has been a delightful study to me. I wish I had time to bring fully to your view, for your consideration, that particular excellence of mind in which he excelled all men that I have ever heard of. I do not mean that his power of forming mechanical combinations was *unlimited,* but that he had it under such perfect *control.* I imagine that he never yet failed of accomplishing any result of mechanical powers and combinations which he sought for ; nor ever sought for one for which he had not some occasion, in order to accomplish the business in hand. I mean that his invention *never failed,* and never *ran wild.* It accomplished, I imagine, without exception, all that he ever asked of it, and *no more.* I emphasize this last expression, from having in mind the case of a man whose invention appeared to be more fertile even than Whitney's ; but he had it under no control. When he had imagined and *half executed* one fine thing, his mind darted off to another, and he perfected nothing : Whitney perfected all that he attempted ; carried each invention to its utmost limit

---

* Hon. S. M. Hopkins.

of usefulness; and then reposed until he had occasion for something else."

It would be difficult to estimate the full value of Mr. Whitney's labors, without going into a minuteness of detail inconsistent with our limits. Every cotton garment bears the impress of his genius, and the ships that transported it across the waters were the heralds of his fame, and the cities that have risen to opulence by the cotton trade, must attribute no small share of their prosperity to the inventor of the cotton gin. We have before us the declaration of the late Mr. Fulton, that Arkwright, Watt and Whitney, (we would add Fulton to the number,) were the three men who did most for mankind, of any of their cotemporaries; and, in the sense in which he intended it, the remark is probably true.

Fabrics of cotton are now so familiar to us and so universally diffused, that we are apt to look upon them rather as original gifts of nature, than as recent products of human ingenuity. The following statements, however, will show how exceedingly limited the cotton trade was previous to the invention of the cotton gin.

In 1784, an American vessel arrived at Liverpool, having on board, for part of her cargo, *eight bags* of cotton, which were seized by the officers of the custom-house, under the conviction that they could not be the growth of America.* The following extracts from old newspapers, will exhibit the extent of the cotton trade for the subsequent years.

Cotton from America arrived at Liverpool.

1785.	January.	*Diana,* from Charleston, 1 bag.
	February.	*Tenign,* from New York, 1 do.
	June.	*Grange,* from Philadelphia, 3 do.—5 bags.
1786.	May.	*Thomas,* from Charleston, 2 do.
	June.	*Juno,* from Charleston, 4 do.—6.
1787.	April.	*John,* from Philadelphia, 6 do.
	June.	*Wilson,* from New York, 9 do.
		Grange, from Philadelphia, 9 do.
	August.	*Henderson,* from Charleston, 40 do.
	Dec.	*John,* from Philadelphia, 44 do.—108.
1788.	January.	*Mersey,* from Charleston, 1 do.
		Grange, from Philadelphia, 5 do.

---

* See Southern Review for May, 1831.

1788.   June.   *John*, from Philadelphia, 30 bags.
        July.   *Harriott*, from New York, 62 do.
                Grange, from Philadelphia, 111 do.
                Polly, from Charleston, 73 do.—282.

The whole domestic exports of the United States in 1825, were valued at 66,940,000 dollars, of which value 36,846,000 was in cotton only. In general, this article is equal to some millions more than one half the whole value of our exports. The average growth for the three years previous to 1828, was estimated at 900,000 bales, which is nearly THREE HUNDRED MILLIONS OF POUNDS, of which about one fifth was consumed in our own manufactories.*

We cannot close this article without adding òne or two reflections that have occurred to us while perusing the papers of Mr. Whitney. President Dwight, in his counsels to his pupils, often insisted on the duty of men of high standing in society, to lend their influence in bringing forward young men of promise ; and no one was ever more ready than that great and good man to take by the hand, and lead forward into the world, young men of modest merit. This noble disposition he manifested strongly in his treatment of the subject of this memoir. He smiled upon his enterprising undertakings, encouraged him by the kindest assurances, and commended him strongly to the countenance and support of his friends. When Mr. W. was about to negotiate a sale of his patent-right with the State of South Carolina, Dr. D. furnished him with a letter to the Hon. Charles Cotesworth Pickney, from which we subjoin the following extract. After adverting to the proposed application of Mr. W., Dr. Dwight proceeds :—" To you, sir, it will be in the stead of many ordinary motives to know that your aid will, in this case, be given to a man who has rarely, perhaps never, been exceeded in ingenuity or industry; and not often in worth of every kind. Every respectable man in this region will rejoice to see him liberally rewarded for so useful an effort, and for a life of uncommon benefit to the public.

" Mr. Whitney is now employed in manufacturing muskets for the United States. In this business he has probably ex-

---

* Niles' Weekly Register.

ceeded the efforts not only of his countrymen, but of the whole civilized world, by a system of machinery of his own invention, in which expedition and accuracy are united to a degree probably without example. I should not have thought it necessary to speak of him in so strong terms, had I not believed that his own modesty would keep him from discovering his real character."

Governor Wolcott, who cherished similar dispositions towards young men of merit and ingenuity, gave him similar letters to Mr. Pickney and Judge Dessaussure. These testimonials no doubt contributed much to inspire confidence in the leading men at the south. Such efforts on the part of eminent men in favor of rising worth, enrich the modest youth without impoverishing themselves.

To a number of respectable gentlemen of New Haven, particularly the Hon. James Hillhouse, the Hon. Elizur Goodrich, the Hon. Simeon Baldwin, and the late Isaac Beers, Esq., Mr. W. was under similar obligations for lending him the credit of their names, and standing sureties for him in the heavy loans which his first great enterprise required, without which aid it could never have been carried forward.

The advantages of a liberal education to a man of mechanical invention, as well as to the man of business, was very conspicuous in the case of Mr. Whitney. By this means his powers of thought, and his materials for combination, were greatly augmented. The letters exchanged between Messrs. Miller & Whitney, both of whom were educated men, are marked by a high degree of intelligence, and are written in a style of great correctness, and sometimes even of elegance. None but men of enlarged and liberal minds could have furnished to their counsel the arguments by which they gained their first triumph over their legal adversaries. It no doubt also contributed not a little to conciliate the respect of those States which purchased the patent-right, to find in the person of the patentee, instead of some illiterate visionary projector, a gentleman of elevated mind and cultivated manners, and of a person elegant and dignified.

In presenting to the public the foregoing sketch of the life of this extraordinary man, the writer has had it constantly in view to render the narrative useful to the enterprising mechanic and the man of business, to whom Whitney may be confidently proposed as a model. To such, it is believed, the details given respecting his various struggles and embarrassments may afford a useful lesson, a fresh incentive to perseverance, and stronger impressions of the value of a character improved by intellectual cultivation, and adorned with all the moral virtues.

REMINISCENCES OF MR. WHITNEY,

BY

PROFESSOR SILLIMAN.

THE preceding memoir has so fully elucidated the character of Mr. Whitney, that the following observations may perhaps appear superfluous. I have, however, been led to make them, both by affection for the memory of a man so highly valued, and also because it is often in the power of a friend to give some additional touches, even to a faithful picture.

Mr. Whitney received the degree of A. B. in Yale College, at the same commencement (1792) when I became a member of that institution. I had only a general knowledge of him until 1798, when I was made acquainted with his then pending arrangement with the government of the United States, for the manufacture of arms, and by request I copied some of the papers relating to that contract. In the autumn of 1799, just after I had accepted an appointment in the government of Yale College, I was much interested by an unexpected application from Mr. Whitney, to visit the principal countries of Europe, (all indeed which had cotton-growing colonies, in either hemisphere,) for the purpose of obtaining patents for the Cotton Gin. Gratifying as the application was to my feelings, my recent engagements with the College, and my youth and inexperience, concurred with other reasons to make me decline accepting the overture, which was sufficiently tempting to my curiosity and to the desire of foreign travel.

This affair would not be worth mentioning, except that the confidence which it implied naturally led to a familiar intercourse of friendship, which for twenty five years was never clouded for a moment, and often gave me interesting views of Mr. Whitney's character.

I was frequently led to observe that his ingenuity extended to every subject which demanded his attention; his arrangements, even of common things, were marked by singular good taste and a prevailing principle of order. The effect of this mental habit is very obvious in the disposition of the buildings and accommodations of his manufactory of arms;—although, owing to the infirmities of his later years, and to other causes, his arrangements were never finished to the full extent of his views. The machinery has great neatness and finish, and in its operation evinces a degree of precision and efficiency which gratifies every curious and intelligent observer. I have many times visited the establishment with strangers and foreigners, who have gone away delighted with what they have seen.* Under all of the successive administrations of the general government, from that of the first President Adams, repeated contracts have been obtained for the supply of arms.

Mr. Whitney received substantial proofs of the approbation of the government in the terms which he obtained. He was personally acquainted with all the Presidents of the United States from the beginning of the government, and in every fluctuation of party he retained their confidence, although his own political sentiments were decided and well known. He was, from frequent and long visits at the seat of government, familiar with the principal officers, and with the leading members of both Houses of Congress; and thus he was enabled to sustain the influence which he had acquired, and even to extend it, so as to obtain important contracts from several of the State governments.

---

* The manufactory has advanced in these respects since it has been superintended by Mr. Whitney's nephews, the Messrs. Blakes, and to them it is indebted for some valuable improvements; and it is at present ably conducted by the son of the founder and inheritor of his name.

The private establishment of Mr. Whitney has proved a a model for the more extensive manufactories which are the property of the nation. Into them, as the writer of the foregoing article has stated, and as I have been informed by Mr. Whitney, his principal improvements have been transplanted, chiefly by the aid of his workmen, and have now become common property.

A few years before Mr. Whitney's death it became necessary to renew the mill-dam at the manufactory; it having been originally constructed for a flour mill, and being both defective in plan and dilapidated by time. Mr. Whitney, then in declining health, superintended every part of the business in person, although its execution was protracted almost into the winter, when massive stones were to be laid, in the midst of cold water and ice. It is necessary only to inspect the work, and the flume ways, and the walled borders of the river below, and the canal which he constructed, to take the water from the dam to the forging shop, to be satisfied that both genius and taste presided over these useful, although unostentatious constructions. The small river, by and upon which they were raised, washes the foot of the celebrated mountain ridge called East Rock, as already mentioned in the preceding memoir. From its precipices and those of one of its branches, which are composed of greenstone trap, Mr. Whitney selected his materials with such skill, and arranged them with such judgment and taste, that the walls, arches, and passages, and some of the shops and other buildings constructed of this rock, are admired both for their solidity and beauty, and will remain to future generations. Some of the works are laid in a cement, composed, in part, of a mixture of iron rust and siliceous and micaceous sand, derived from the grinding of the gun-barrels and other pieces of iron upon the grindstones—a cement which appears almost as firm as the rocks themselves. There are two buildings for fuel : the one for charcoal, and the other for mineral coal ; both are finished with great exactness, by selecting smooth natural faces of the trap rock, which are accurately laid in mortar and carefully pointed ; the floors are also of firm stone, laid with equal exactness. These store-houses stand by the side of the mountain and at its foot, and by excavating a road in the bank above, the coal carts are driven quite up to the gable end of the building, and their loads are discharged into them simply by tipping up the cart. This notice of these humble buildings is given to show Mr. Whitney's exactness in every thing. It was a maxim with him, which I have often heard him repeat, that *there is nothing worth doing that is not worth doing well.* As far as circumstances permitted, he always acted up to this maxim.

The houses for his workmen, at the manufactory, are beautifully constructed, and arranged upon one plan ; they also are of trap rock,* and covered by a white cement, and together with the other buildings, the mountain and river scenery, and the bridge,† they give this picturesque valley no small degree of beauty. It was Mr. Whitney's intention to erect his own mansion house in this valley, which would doubtless have then received all the embellishment of which it is so susceptible. With this view he had constructed an ample barn,‡ which is a model of convenience, and even of taste and beauty, and contains many accommodations, not usually found in such establishments. It was visited and examined by the late President Monroe, during his excursion through the Eastern States, in 1816. It is perfectly characteristic of Mr. Whitney, that his attention was directed even to the mangers for the cattle, and to their fastenings. The latter are so contrived, by means of a small weight at the end of the halter, that the animal could always move his head with facility, but could not draw out the rope so as to become entangled in it, nor could he easily waste his hay. The fastenings of the doors, as well as all the other appendages and accommodations, are equally ingenious.

The great water wheels which move the machinery of the manufactory, are constructed entirely of wrought iron, combining the greatest strength, durability and beauty, with a pro-

---

* Since Mr. Whitney's death, other houses have been built of wood.
† Constructed by that ingenious architect, Mr. Ithiel Town.
‡ There is a farm connected with the manufactory.

jectile power like that of the fly-wheels in steam engines.
They are elegant objects, especially when in motion.

Mr. Whitney did not forget the domestic arrangements of
his own house, which contained many specimens of that ingenuity which he evinced in common things, as well as in those
that are more important. The several drawers of his bureaus
were locked by a single movement of one key, of a peculiar
construction, and an attempt to open any drawer except one
would prove ineffectual, even with the right key, which, however, being applied in the proper place, threw all the bolts at
one movement. These bureaus are now in the house of Mrs.
Whitney.

During the decline of his health, and especially during his
severest attacks, I was with him almost daily, and saw how
intensely his powerful and acute mind was directed to his own
case, of which he made himself perfect master.* It has been
already stated in the memoir, that his health was subverted,
and his life ultimately terminated by a very painful local affection,† brought on, as he informed me, by exposure and fatigue during the last of his land journeys through North Carolina, on his way to Georgia, to assert his just claims, so long
and so injuriously frustrated.‡ He examined with great care
and coolness the best medical writers on his disease; he in-
spected their plates; conversed freely with his professional

---

* Such was the remark made to him by one of the greatest surgeons of this country, who, after a painful examination in one of the great cities, gave him no encouragement to hope for any permanent relief.

† Not only of the prostate gland, but of the vicinal organs; this was the fatal
disease of Mr. Whitney's illustrious friend, the late President Dwight. Thus were
removed most painfully, from life, two of the greatest and most useful men which
this country has produced.

‡ He made many journeys to Georgia on this painful business, and generally by
land, in an open sulkey. Near the close of life, he said in my hearing, that all he
had received for the invention of the cotton gin, had not more than compensated
him for the enormous expenses which he had incurred, and for the time which he
had devoted during many of the best years of his life, in the prosecution of this subject. He therefore felt that his just claims on the cotton-growing States, especially
on those that had made him no returns for this invention, so important to his country, were still unsatisfied, and that both justice and honor required that compensation
should be made.

advisers, who withheld nothing from him, and he was not satisfied without such anatomical illustrations as were furnished from the museum of an eminent professor of anatomy. He critically recorded such facts in his case as interested him the most, and in coolness and decision, acted rather as if he himself had been the physician than the patient.

During this period, embracing at intervals several years, he devised and caused to be constructed various instruments, for his own personal use, the minute description of which would not be appropriate to this place. Nothing that he ever invented, not even the cotton gin, discovered a more perfect comprehension of the difficulties to be surmounted, or evinced more efficient ingenuity in the accomplishment of his object. Such was his resolution and perseverance, that from his sick chamber he wrote both to London and Paris, for materials important to his plans, and he lived to receive the things he required, and to apply them in the way that he had intended. He was perfectly successful, so far as any mechanical means could afford relief or palliation; but his terrible malady bore down his constitution, by repeated, and eventually by incessant inroads, upon the powers of life, which at last yielded to assaults which no human means could avert or sustain. One of the important inventions of that distressing period is in the possession of the artist who was employed to construct the instrument,* but it is to be feared that other contrivances, remarkable for their simplicity and efficiency, as well as originality, are but imperfectly remembered by the friends and attendants. I urged Mr. Whitney, and the late Dr. Smith, his attending physician, to make sure of these inventions while it was possible, but I believe no record was ever made of them, and it is but too probable that the instruments are lost.

I have mentioned these facts connected with Mr. Whitney's last illness, merely as instances of his never-sleeping ingenuity and mental acuteness, rendered still more active, without being enfeebled, by intense suffering.

I have seen the same traits manifested on occasions far less

---

* Mr. Deming.

important, but to him, at the time, equally novel. In the summer of 1808, application was made by myself and others, to Mr. Whitney, for tubes of block tin, for the purpose of drawing through an innocuous metal, the soda water* highly charged with carbonic acid gas. Lead and copper tubes were rejected on account of their poisonous properties, and there were then no facilities in this country for constructing the tubes that were desired. Mr. Whitney accomplished the object, with his usual precision. The tubes were required to be many feet long, and strong enough to resist a heavy pressure. He caused a mould to be constructed of cast brass, in two parts, each containing for about two feet in length, one half of the cylindrical cavity, corresponding to the desired tube. When the parts of the mould were accurately fitted, by their faces, and screwed together, they contained the entire cylindrical cavity between them, and to secure the duct through the tube, a polished steel rod, of the proper size, and made very slightly tapering, was fixed in the centre and the melted metal was cast around it ; the rod, being terminated by a ring, was easily knocked out. The separate parts of the tube, thus produced, were then joined into one, by having the contiguous ends of two of them brought longitudinally into contact, and included in another mould, containing an enlarged cavity, into which melted tin was poured. The duct was preserved by a steel rod passing through it as before, and thus the joint was perfected by a knob of metal, which at once united the two tubes into one, gave them great additional strength, and furnished a beautiful ornament. Nothing could be more perfect for the object. The moulds are still in existence, and were it necessary, tubes could be thus made a mile long. Mr. Whitney did not state that this method was original, nor do I certainly know whether it was ; but I have never heard of a similar method of casting block tin tubes. Mr. Whitney considered it as so valuable, that he chose to pay for the moulds, although they were expensive, and he retained them with reference to future use for himself.

---

* Then just beginning to be known in this country.

The operations of Mr. Whitney's mind were not so remarkable for rapidity as for precision. This arose, not from the want of mental activity and ardor of feeling, but from habitual caution, and from his having made it his rule to be satisfied with nothing short of perfection. Hence, he delayed to mention a projected invention or improvement until he was entirely satisfied with his own views. He did not disclose them until, in his own opinion, he had hit upon the best conception and the best means of execution, and when these were attained, and not before, he brought his project forward, or, more frequently, put it into successful operation before he divulged his plan. Hence, he rarely found it necessary to retrace his steps. In early life he so effectually disciplined his mind, that he could not only confine it to the contemplation of one subject, but he could suspend his train of thought and the execution of his inventions, and resume them at distant intervals without confusion or loss. He was very patient of interruption, and would cheerfully leave his own engagements and suspend his mechanical arrangements, his repasts, or his business, to attend to the 'numerous applications which were constantly made to him, both by those who had, and those who had not, any proper claims to his time and services.

No man, as stated in the memoir, knew better how to control the excursions of an inventive mind. I have heard him speak feelingly of the ruin often brought by ingenious men upon themselves, by allowing their minds to wander from invention to invention; devising many things and completing nothing; and he considered it equally his own duty and interest to adhere inflexibly to those undertakings which he could carry into successful operation, and to deny himself the luxury of a perpetual mental creation.

With all his contemplative ingenuity and habitual attention to mechanical details, Mr. Whitney did not allow his mind to be narrowed down to a limited horizon. His views of men and things were on the most enlarged scale. The interests of mankind, and especially of his native country, as connected with government, liberty, order, science, arts, literature, morals, and religion, were familiar to his mind, and he delighted in conversing with men of a similar character.

His amiable and generous dispositions also prompted him strongly to social intercourse. His countenance and person were so prepossessing as to excite an active interest, especially whenever he spoke ; his gentlemanly manners, marked by a calm, but dignified modesty, were still those of a man not unconscious of his own mental powers ; he was therefore self-possessed, while a winning affability and an agreeable voice made his conversation as attractive as it was instructive. He abounded in information and in original thoughts ; he was always welcome in the best society, both at home and when he traveled ; the first men of the country, and from almost every State in the Union, called on him, and much of his time was necessarily passed in society. Before he had a family, his carriage was often observed standing, till a late hour in the evening, at the doors of some of his friends, and he seemed reluctantly to withdraw to his manufactory, which was two miles from the town. Mr. Whitney was constant and warm in his friendships, and his efficient pecuniary aid, (after he came to be possessed of the means,) was often afforded not only to his friends, but to persons who had sometimes no claims except those that addressed themselves to his kindness and generosity. Those who relied upon these traits were rarely disappointed, but he did not consider himself as being always requited, either with substantial justice or with gratitude ; a case which is, however, not altogether singular in the world. Many thousands of dollars, amounting to a considerable fortune, were lost to Mr. Whitney, through his generosity.

It is perhaps worthy of being mentioned, that Mr. Whitney's amiable dispositions and power of pleasing were manifested in the pleasure which he took in caressing children, and in the ease with which he won their attachment. In my own family, as a visiting friend, he always allured the children, at once, around him, and neither he nor they were soon tired of the little gambols and pastimes started for their amusement. Such happy dispositions eminently fitted him for the high domestic happiness which he found in his own family, during the few years that he was permitted to enjoy their society. After he became convinced that he could not survive his disease, he manifested a wise prospective forecast for their welfare; and it is characteristic of his peculiar turn of mind, that the ample house which, had he lived, he had intended to erect, he ordered to be built after his death, for his lady and their children. His fortitude and sense of decorum never forsook him during his long and distressing decline. He almost always saw his friends, and some of them he would never suffer to be denied ; even when in intense pain, he was cheerful, social, courteous, and, to the last, he maintained the observance of order and proper attention to his person. He desired that the writer of these notes should be in the house at the closing scene ; and although this was prevented by circumstances, he expressed to him, near the close of life, sentiments such as we should wish to hear from a dying friend. As is common in cases where there has been severe suffering, his countenance, after death, assumed its natural expression, even in a greater degree than for several weeks before.

His funeral was attended by a large concourse of his fellow citizens, who assembled in one of the churches, to which the body was conveyed, and where an appropriate religious service was performed.

His tomb is after the model of that of Scipio at Rome, a miniature of which, of the same stone of which it was originally made, was sent out cut from Italy by Mr. William C. Woodbridge, and has been adopted in the case of two other eminent men, the late Dr. Nathan Smith, and Mr. Ashmun, the founder of the colony of Liberia. It is simple, beautiful, and grand, and promises to endure for centuries.* An accurate drawing of it, by Mr. R. Bakewell, Jr., is annexed.

---

* The foundations of the monument are laid at the bottom of the grave, by the sides of the coffin, and depressed below it ; an arch of stone is thrown over the coffin, and the structure then rises, solid as an ancient temple. The material of the monument is the fine grained sandstone, of Chatham, Conn. The several layers of stone are composed each of one piece only.

The following observations of a distinguished scholar and statesman, elicited in consequence of a recent visit to the cemetery of New Haven, evince the estimation

On Mr. Whitney's tomb is the following inscription :

ELI WHITNEY,

The inventor of the Cotton Gin.

Of useful Science and Arts, the efficient Patron and Improver.

In the social relations of life, a Model of excellence.

While private affection weeps at his tomb, his country honors his memory.

Born Dec. 8, 1765.—Died Jan. 8, 1825.

---

in which Mr. Whitney's name is held, by one who is fully capable of appreciating his merits. After alluding to the monument of Gen. Humphreys, who introduced the fine wooled sheep into this country, the stranger remarks :—" But Whitney's monument perpetuates the name of a still greater public benefactor. His simple name would have been epitaph enough, with the addition perhaps of ' the inventor of the cotton gin.' How few of the inscriptions in Westminster Abbey could be compared with that ! Who is there that, like him, has given his country a machine—the product of his own skill—which has furnished a large part of its population, ' from childhood to age, with a lucrative employment ; by which their debts have been paid off ; their capitals increased ; *their lands trebled in value.'** It may be said indeed that this belongs to the physical and material nature of man, and ought not to be compared with what has been done by the intellectual benefactors of mankind—the Miltons, the Shakspeares, and the Newtons. But is it quite certain that any thing short of the highest intellectual vigor—the brightest genius—is sufficient to invent one of these extraordinary machines? Place a common mind before an oration of Cicero and a steam engine, and it will despair of rivaling the latter as much as the former ; and we can by no means be persuaded, that the peculiar aptitude for combining and applying the simple powers of mechanics, so as to produce these marvelous operations, does not imply a vivacity of the imagination, not inferior to that of the poet and the orator. And then, as to the effect on society, the machine, it is true, operates, in the first instance, on mere physical elements, to produce an accumulation and distribution of property. But do not all the arts of civilization follow in the train? and has not he who has trebled the value of land, created capital, rescued the population from the necessity of emigrating, and covered a waste with plenty—has not he done a service to the country of the highest moral and intellectual character? Prosperity is the parent of civilization, and all its refinements ; and every family of prosperous citizens added to the community, is an addition of so many thinking, inventing, moral and immortal natures."—*New England Magazine,* Nov. 1831.

* The words of Mr. Justice Johnson of South Carolina, in the opinion in the case of Whitney *versus* Carter.

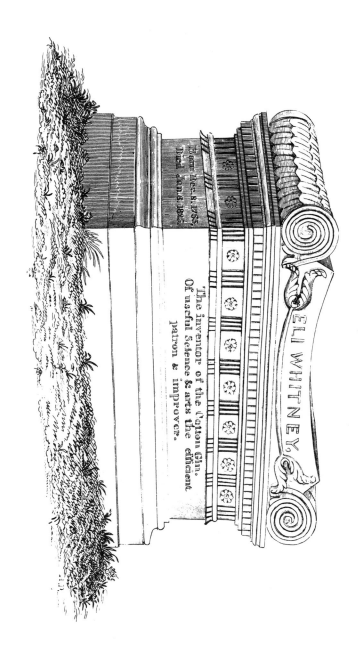

ELI WHITNEY.

The inventor of the Cotton Gin.
Of useful Science & arts the efficient
patron & improver.

Born Dec. 8, 1765.
Died Jan. 8, 1825.

APPENDIX.

The Effect of the Invention of the Cotton-Gin on the Production of Cotton.

THE influence of mechanical inventions on the improvement of the human race, and the wealth of nations, is a circumstance which has peculiarly impressed the minds of practical men and of philosophic observers alike, since the beginning of the nineteenth century. Changes in the condition of society and in the intercourse of nations, far more momentous and lasting than the revolutions previously produced by political causes, have, within the last fifty years, been effected by the action of individual minds, in the development of neglected physical facts, and in the application of material agencies to the use and benefit of man. As new wants have been felt, and the needed uses of yet undiscovered powers have been made known in the progress of society, art and science have met each occasion ; and the demand for new combinations of matter and motion has been continually answered by widely-various, unwearied invention.

The application of steam to machinery, to navigation and to land carriage, the invention of the spinning-frame, and of the cotton-gin, are imposing instances of the operation of such causes, so insignificant in their inception, so immensely important in their results, to the convenience and happiness of mankind. The agency of Watt, Fulton, Stevens, Telford, Arkwright, and Whitney, in the production of the present wealth of the world, and in the development of the before-unappreciated resources of the rapidly improving commonwealths and empires of progressive Christendom, has been greater than that of all other human causes. What may have been accomplished by government, by policy and by science, for the promotion of the general good of civilized nations, is little in comparison with the production of these individual minds acting wholly without the sphere of political agencies, and has been wholly subordinate and secondary to it.

These views of the relative influence and importance of merely personal, private agency, and of national or governmental movements, would have startled the world in the last century, and would have received a contemptuous condemnation ; but to the present generation, they have been made familiar by reiteration, almost to triteness.

The increase of the production of a cheap material for woven fabrics, adapted in some degree to the use of the human race in every climate and region, is a matter of more importance to commerce and to the interests of civilization, than may appear to a superficial observer. The supply of this primary necessity of man, (hardly less essential than that of food,) with an article capable of being substituted, to a great extent, for every other material hitherto converted into cloth, has been, during the present half-century, by far the most important element in the commercial relations of the United States and Europe,—has been the source of the largest amount of acquired wealth, and has given employment to the greatest aggregate of profitable labor. There is no parallel in history to the changes which the cotton trade has made in the direction of commerce, in the employment of mechanical industry, in the dress, habits, conveniences, and health of mankind, and in the intercourse and mutual dependence of nations. And when it is remembered, that the material was, by the invention of the COTTON-GIN, furnished to the manufacturer with the cheapness, abundance and dispatch which insured these great results, it becomes manifest that the importance of this mechanism has not been overrated.

The memoir, which this statement accompanies, furnishes some facts relating to the consequences of Mr. Whitney's invention to the growth of cotton ; but the increase of the production, manufacture, and exportation of that great American staple during the years which have intervened, has created a necessity for an extended view of the statistics of the subject. The limits of the present sketch permit only an outline or abstract of the facts. It is a topic which has largely employed the faculties of commercial writers and statesmen in the United States and in Great Britain, the results of whose labors may be obtained from the public documents of the American government, and from the various volumes of Hunt's " Merchants' Magazine,"—a periodical of great merit and value for commercial statistics of this and similar character.

Numerous statistical tables have been published in works of this description, exhibiting the annual cultivation of cotton in the different States of the Union and throughout the world, and also showing the amount and value of the exportations of cotton from the United States to the various countries of Europe. The influence of the cotton-gin on the increase and relative amount of American production and exportation, is thus exhibited by a statement of the growth here and elsewhere, in certain years, at fixed periods.

Tables, exhibiting at great length all the particulars of production and export, for each year, from 1791 to the present time, are given in several articles in Hunt's " Merchants' Magazine," especially in a History of the American Cotton Trade, by JAMES H. LANMAN, in Vol. IV, page 201, of that work. A document prepared by the Treasury Department in 1836, in obedience to a resolution passed in Congress, presents also very ample and valuable tabular details of the progress of the cotton trade and culture for more than forty years. The Merchants' Magazine contains also a very valuable series of articles on this subject, (by Professor M'Cay, of the University of Georgia,) presenting minute statements of the annual production and exportation of cotton during recent years. (Merchants' Magazine, Vol. IX, p. 516 ; Vol. XI, p. 517 ; Vol. XIII, p. 507.) From these, most of the particulars here given are derived ; and to these and the American Almanac for 1837, and to the Annual Reports on Commerce and Navigation prepared by the Treasury Department, the inquiring reader is referred for the complete statistics of the agriculture, commerce and manufacture of cotton.

The grand results, however, may be viewed effectively from a few points of time, selecting the statistics of certain dates, taken at random. In the year 1791, the whole cotton crop of the United States was but 2,000,000 of pounds. In 1845, (fifty-two years after the invention of the cotton-gin,) it was more than 1,000,000,000 of pounds, (2,395,000 bales, averaging above 430 pounds.) In 1791, the cotton annually produced in the whole world was estimated at 490,000,000 lbs., of which the United States, consequently, produced only $\frac{1}{245}$. In 1845, the total supply furnished in the markets of the civilized world, was 1,169,600,000 lbs., (2,720,000 bales,) of which the United States produced, therefore, more than SEVEN-EIGHTHS.

In 1791, the whole amount of cotton exported from the United States was 189,316 pounds,—this being the first definite statement of the kind on record. Previous to that year, the growth and sale of cotton had been so trifling in amount, as to be accounted unworthy of any notice in the statistics of American commerce, or even in those of Southern agriculture. Although it is known that even in 1770 there were shipped to Liverpool, THREE bales of cotton from New York, FOUR bales from Virginia and Maryland, and THREE from North Carolina—and though, in 1784, (the year after the Treaty which closed the Revolutionary War and secured the recognition of American Independence by Great Britain,) a vessel that carried EIGHT bales of cotton from the United States to Liverpool was seized in that port, on the ground that *so large a quantity of* COTTON in a single cargo could not be the produce of the United States,—yet there was no decisive improvement in the production or exportation of this article down to the era of Whitney's invention. And in 1792, (the year preceding the invention,) the quantity *exported* was even less than in 1791, amounting only to 138,328 lbs.—a *decrease* of 50,988 lbs. in one year. There was no indication, from 1770 to 1792, of any tendency to a large increase of the production of cotton ; and however great the adaptation of the soil and climate of the South to its culture, and however strong the encouragements afforded by the extended demand and high price in Britain and on the European continent, no one, at that time, seems to have expected that this was ever to be one of the great staples and exports of the United States.

In 1793, the year of the invention, the whole cotton crop of the United States was 5,000,000 lbs., and the total *exportation* 487,600 lbs. In 1794, when the cotton-gin was first extensively introduced into Georgia and South Carolina, (then the principal region of that production,) the whole crop increased to 8,000,000 lbs., and the exportation to 1,601,760 lbs. In 1800, when the machine had been thrown open to the people, without limitation, from regard to the legal rights of the patentee, the total production of cotton in the United States, during the year, amounted to 35,000,000 lbs., of which 17,789,803 lbs. were exported. In 1805, the whole production was 70,000,000 lbs., and the amount of *upland* cotton exported, 29,602,428 lbs. —(value, $9,445,000.) In 1810, the crop was increased to 85,000,000 lbs., and the exportation of *upland* cotton to 84,657,384 lbs. In 1815, the whole of the United States crop was 100,000,000 lbs., and the exportation of *upland* cotton 74,548,796 lbs. In 1820, the whole United States crop was 160,000,000 lbs.—the exportation of *upland* 116,291,137 lbs., valued at $22,308,667. In 1825, crop 255,000,000 lbs. —exportation of *upland*, 166,784,629 lbs. In 1830, crop 350,000,000,—exportation, 290,311,937. In 1835, crop 475,000,000—exportation, 379,000,000. In 1840, crop 880,000,000—exportation valued at $63,870,307. In 1845, the United States cotton crop was 1,029,850,000 pounds, and the exportation of cotton 862,580,000 pounds—the domestic consumption being 167,270,000 pounds.

The recent annexation of the immense cotton-lands of Texas, the abolition of the import duty on American cotton in Great Britain, and the vast and rapid increase of the manufacture of cotton-fabrics in all parts of the United States, are evidences of the certainty of a further increase in the production of cotton in this country. Enormous as has been the progress of this staple, from 1791 to 1845, it is destined to a yet greater extension in amount and value.

The exclusion of East India cotton from its previous monopoly of the markets of the civilized world, from the beginning of the present century, was mainly due to the introduction of the cotton-gin in the Southern States of the American Union, which substituted the rapid operations of machinery for the tedious and costly labor of human hands in the preparation of the crop for the use of the manufacturer. The recent attempts of the British Government and the East India Company to restore the successful production of cotton in Hindostan, have consisted largely in the introduction of American improvements, especially of "THE AMERICAN COTTON-GIN," into those provinces which are adapted to the culture. The greater cheapness of labor, and even the superior quality of the product (in the province of Dharwar) were found to avail nothing, without the advantages of American machinery.

The pecuniary advantage of this invention to the United States is by no means fully presented by an exhibition of the value of the exports of cotton, (amounting to more than $1,400,000,000 in the last forty-three years,) nor by the immense proportion of the means which it has furnished this country to meet the enormous debts continually incurred for imports from Britain and the European continent—COTTON having for many years constituted $\frac{1}{2}$, $\frac{3}{5}$, or $\frac{7}{10}$ of the value of the exports of the Union. But it was the introduction of the cotton-gin which first gave a high value and permanent market to the Public Lands in the southwest. The rapid settlement and improvement of almost the entire States of Alabama, Mississippi, Louisiana, Florida, and Texas, is mainly due to the enlarged production of cotton consequent upon the invention of Whitney. The States of Georgia and Tennessee have also been largely benefited by the same means, in the disposal of their domain, a vast portion of which must have remained unoccupied and valueless but for the immense increase of facilities for the preparation of cotton for the market. In the three States of Alabama, Mississippi, and Louisiana, the sales of the public lands of the General Government amounted to 18,099,505 acres, during the eleven years ending on the thirtieth of June, 1844,—yielding to the National Treasury more than $30,000,000. The sales of upland cotton lands by the United States land-offices, have amounted to many tens of millions of acres; and none have been sold at a lower rate than $1.25 an acre—a large proportion at a higher rate.

It is to be remarked, finally, that the cotton-gins now in use throughout the whole South are truly the original invention of Whitney,—that no improvement or successful variation of the essential parts has yet been effected. The actual characteristics of the machine, (the cylinder and brush,) the sole real instruments by which the seed is removed and the cotton cleaned, REMAIN, in cotton-gins of even the most recent manufacture, PRECISELY AS WHITNEY LEFT THEM. The *principle* has not been altered since the first cotton-gin was put in motion by the inventor, though great improvements have been made in the application and direction of the moving forces, in the employment of steam-power, in the running-gear, and other incidentals. Every one of the various cotton-gins in use, under the names of different makers, contains the essentials of Whitney's patent, without material change or addition. The brush and the cylinder remain, like Fulton's paddle-wheel, unchanged in form and necessity, however vast the improvements in the machinery that causes the motion.

A more imposing result of mechanical ingenuity directed to the benefit of a whole nation, and, through it, of mankind, has not been recorded in the history of the human mind. Certainly there is no patriotic American that will not rejoice to accord to this eminently useful, though basely-wronged inventor, the judgment so well expressed by Mr. Lanman, (Merchant's Magazine, Vol. IV, pp. 208, 209,)—that " Whitney earned the credit of giving a spring to the agriculture of the South, which has been continued, unimpaired, to this day,—a credit that will endure while the cotton-plant whitens the plantations of the South with its snowy harvests, or the machinery of the cotton-factory clatters upon the waterfall!"

TECHNOLOGY AND SOCIETY

An Arno Press Collection

Ardrey, R[obert] L. **American Agricultural Implements.** In two parts. 1894

Arnold, Horace Lucien and Fay Leone Faurote. **Ford Methods and the Ford Shops.** 1915

Baron, Stanley [Wade]. **Brewed in America:** A History of Beer and Ale in the United States. 1962

Bathe, Greville and Dorothy. **Oliver Evans:** A Chronicle of Early American Engineering. 1935

Bendure, Zelma and Gladys Pfeiffer. **America's Fabrics:** Origin and History, Manufacture, Characteristics and Uses. 1946

Bichowsky, F. Russell. **Industrial Research.** 1942

Bigelow, Jacob. **The Useful Arts:** Considered in Connexion with the Applications of Science. 1840. Two volumes in one

Birkmire, William H. **Skeleton Construction in Buildings.** 1894

Boyd, T[homas] A[lvin]. **Professional Amateur:** The Biography of Charles Franklin Kettering. 1957

Bright, Arthur A[aron], Jr. **The Electric-Lamp Industry:** Technological Change and Economic Development from 1800 to 1947. 1949

Bruce, Alfred and Harold Sandbank. **The History of Prefabrication.** 1943

Carr, Charles C[arl]. **Alcoa, An American Enterprise.** 1952

Cooley, Mortimer E. **Scientific Blacksmith.** 1947

Davis, Charles Thomas. **The Manufacture of Paper.** 1886

Deane, Samuel. **The New-England Farmer,** or Georgical Dictionary. 1822

Dyer, Henry. **The Evolution of Industry.** 1895

Epstein, Ralph C. **The Automobile Industry:** Its Economic and Commercial Development. 1928

Ericsson, Henry. **Sixty Years a Builder:** The Autobiography of Henry Ericsson. 1942

Evans, Oliver. **The Young Mill-Wright and Miller's Guide.** 1850

Ewbank, Thomas. **A Descriptive and Historical Account of Hydraulic and Other Machines for Raising Water,** Ancient and Modern. 1842

Field, Henry M. **The Story of the Atlantic Telegraph.** 1893

Fleming, A. P. M. **Industrial Research in the United States of America.** 1917

Van Gelder, Arthur Pine and Hugo Schlatter. **History of the Explosives Industry in America.** 1927

Hall, Courtney Robert. **History of American Industrial Science.** 1954

Hungerford, Edward. **The Story of Public Utilities.** 1928

Hungerford, Edward. **The Story of the Baltimore and Ohio Railroad, 1827-1927.** 1928

Husband, Joseph. **The Story of the Pullman Car.** 1917

Ingels, Margaret. **Willis Haviland Carrier, Father of Air Conditioning.** 1952

Kingsbury, J[ohn] E. **The Telephone and Telephone Exchanges:** Their Invention and Development. 1915

Labatut, Jean and Wheaton J. Lane, eds. **Highways in Our National Life:** A Symposium. 1950

Lathrop, William G[ilbert]. **The Brass Industry in the United States.** 1926

Lesley, Robert W., John B. Lober and George S. Bartlett. **History of the Portland Cement Industry in the United States.** 1924

Marcosson, Isaac F. **Wherever Men Trade:** The Romance of the Cash Register. 1945

Miles, Henry A[dolphus]. **Lowell, As It Was, and As It Is.** 1845

Morison, George S. **The New Epoch:** As Developed by the Manufacture of Power. 1903

Olmsted, Denison. **Memoir of Eli Whitney, Esq.** 1846

Passer, Harold C. **The Electrical Manufacturers, 1875-1900.** 1953

Prescott, George B[artlett]. **Bell's Electric Speaking Telephone.** 1884

Prout, Henry G. **A Life of George Westinghouse.** 1921

Randall, Frank A. **History of the Development of Building Construction in Chicago.** 1949

Riley, John J. **A History of the American Soft Drink Industry:** Bottled Carbonated Beverages, 1807-1957. 1958

Salem, F[rederick] W[illiam]. **Beer, Its History and Its Economic Value as a National Beverage.** 1880

Smith, Edgar F. **Chemistry in America.** 1914

Steinman, D[avid] B[arnard]. **The Builders of the Bridge:** The Story of John Roebling and His Son. 1950

Taylor, F[rank] Sherwood. **A History of Industrial Chemistry.** 1957

Technological Trends and National Policy, Including the Social Implications of New Inventions. Report of the Subcommittee on Technology to the National Resources Committee. 1937

Thompson, John S. **History of Composing Machines.** 1904

Thompson, Robert Luther. **Wiring a Continent:** The History of the Telegraph Industry in the United States, 1832-1866. 1947

Tilley, Nannie May. **The Bright-Tobacco Industry, 1860-1929.** 1948

Tooker, Elva. **Nathan Trotter:** Philadelphia Merchant, 1787-1853. 1955

Turck, J. A. V. **Origin of Modern Calculating Machines.** 1921

Tyler, David Budlong. **Steam Conquers the Atlantic.** 1939

Wheeler, Gervase. **Homes for the People,** In Suburb and Country. 1855